ASSUMPTION-BASED
PLANNING

A PLANNING TOOL FOR VERY UNCERTAIN TIMES

James A. Dewar
Carl H. Builder
William M. Hix
Morlie H. Levin

Prepared for the
United States Army

RAND

This report documents a strategic planning methodology, Assumption-Based Planning, that RAND has developed over the last four years. It distills long-range planning work for the Training and Doctrine Command (TRADOC) Research Activity and the Manpower, Training, and Performance Program (now the Manpower and Training Program) of RAND's Arroyo Center and was funded as Arroyo Center exploratory research.

This work was conducted to aid the U.S. Army with its long- and mid-range planning. As argued, the method is particularly suited to planning in the military. It should also be of interest to anyone engaged in long-range or strategic planning. This report is intended to describe the fundamentals of Assumption-Based Planning and to provide numerous examples, although it is not a complete user's manual.

THE ARROYO CENTER

The Arroyo Center is the U.S. Army's federally funded research and development center (FFRDC) for studies and analysis operated by RAND. The Arroyo Center provides the Army with objective, independent analytic research on major policy and organizational concerns, emphasizing mid- and long-term problems. Its research is carried out in four programs: Strategy and Doctrine, Force Development and Technology, Military Logistics, and Manpower and Training.

Army Regulation 5-21 contains basic policy for the conduct of the Arroyo Center. The Army provides continuing guidance and oversight through the Arroyo Center Policy Committee (ACPC), which is co-chaired by the Vice Chief of Staff and by the Assistant Secretary for Research, Development, and Acquisition. Arroyo Center work is performed under contract MDA903-91-C-0006.

The Arroyo Center is housed in RAND's Army Research Division. RAND is a private, nonprofit institution that conducts analytic research on a wide range of public policy matters affecting the nation's security and welfare.

Lynn E. Davis is Vice President for the Army Research Division and the Director of the Arroyo Center. Those interested in further information about the Arroyo Center should contact her office directly:

Lynn E. Davis
RAND
1700 Main Street
P.O. Box 2138
Santa Monica, CA 90407-2138

CONTENTS

FIGURES

TABLES

National security planning in the recent past has typically been based on a most-likely future world extrapolated from current trends. In a stable, predictable world, such as during the Cold War era, such a planning approach is reasonable. However, during very uncertain times, such as those of today, no single future world is very likely. Plans that assume the likelihood of one particular world run the risk of being seriously wrong.

Another approach, first developed for long-range planning in the Army, is to begin with what can be known—the assumptions on which current operations or plans are based. The task then is to identify those assumptions that are vulnerable to failure in the time frame of planning interest. For such assumptions, signposts can be developed to monitor their vulnerability and actions can be defined both to protect the assumptions and to prepare for the possibility that they may fail in any event.

In times of great uncertainty, such an approach is more accommodating of a wide variety of potential changes in the world, and its outputs help produce more robust, resilient plans. The challenges in this approach are to identify the critical assumptions underlying an organization's thinking and operations, and then to understand which of those assumptions may become vulnerable and how.

Over the last four years, RAND has developed and tested such an approach, called Assumption-Based Planning (ABP). ABP can be codified in the following five basic steps.

STEP 1: IDENTIFY IMPORTANT ASSUMPTIONS

An *assumption* in this context is an assertion about some characteristic of the future that underlies the current operations or plans of an
organization. An assumption is *important* if its negation would lead
to significant changes in those operations or plans.

It is a rare organization that explicitly sets out all the important assumptions it has made. More typically, those assumptions must be
identified from documentation, interviews, and observation. Even
when such assumptions are written down explicitly, unstated, implicit assumptions remain to be identified and are evident only upon
reflection and study.

Identifying an organization's important explicit and implicit assumptions is a useful exercise in itself as a way of clarifying an
organization's identity and mission.

STEP 2: IDENTIFY ASSUMPTION VULNERABILITIES

An organization's assumptions are not immutable facts but, rather,
are projected to hold true for some period of time. The *planning
time horizon* is the farthest point out that a given planning effort will
consider; it sets the limits on the vulnerability of an assumption. In
some cases, an organization's planning time horizon is set before
planning begins. If not, it *must* be set before vulnerabilities can be
established.

To determine which assumptions may be vulnerable within the
planning time horizon, one must identify elements of change that
indicate what could happen in the world within that horizon. These
are not predictions. An *element of change* is an event or world condition that (1) represents change from today, (2) is plausible within
the planning horizon, and (3) is related to the organization and its
plans. Futures research provides a variety of means for identifying
such elements of change.

What makes an assumption vulnerable are those elements of change
that would violate the assumption or cause it to be wrong. In general, an assumption may be violated in more than one way, and it is
important to capture that variety.

STEP 3: DEFINE SIGNPOSTS

A *signpost* is an event or threshold that clearly indicates the changing vulnerability of an assumption. Signposts are critical to Assumption-Based Planning, which is driven by the notion that the best approach in an uncertain planning environment is to do what needs doing now and to watch for changes that will resolve the uncertainties in the future. Signposts are the mechanism for monitoring the uncertainties in the organization's future, and they play a role in determining when to perform shaping and hedging actions.

The fundamental challenge in defining signposts is to ensure that the indications are unambiguous and not the product of a deliberate attempt to mislead.

STEP 4: DEFINE SHAPING ACTIONS

A *shaping action* is an organizational action designed either to avert or to cause the failure of a vulnerable assumption. For a given vulnerable assumption, this step entails deciding whether a potential change in that assumption is for the better or the worse, identifying the extent to which the organization has control over the assumption, and defining actions to exert that control.

STEP 5: DEFINE HEDGING ACTIONS

A *hedging action* is an organizational action intended to better prepare an organization for the failure of one of its important assumptions. Fundamentally different from a shaping action, a hedging action requires an act of replanning. Defining hedging actions requires rethinking an organization's plans *as though* an important assumption had failed, and it ascribes certainty to a failure that is only plausible. In so doing, it enables exploration of actions the organization can take now to preserve important options in light of the plausibility of that assumption's failing at some point.

Although there are alternative methods for exploring the implications of a failed, or violated, assumption, we recommend developing a fictitious but plausible world with that failed assumption in it and then exploring that world—an approach that has the advantages of putting the failed assumption into a realistic context and of generating interest from others in contemplating responses.

ORDERING OF THE ABP STEPS

To order the steps of Assumption-Based Planning is to suggest that, logically, ABP is a sequential process, with each step depending on the previous one. This is not the case. Steps 3, 4, and 5 depend logically on the sequential completion of Steps 1 and 2, but the information available after Step 2 is sufficient to undertake any of the last three steps, which may be done in any order or even in parallel.

There is, however, a dimension along which the steps, as ordered, represent a monotonic change. At one end of this dimension is "how to think" about the future; at the other is "what to do" about it. In order, the steps of ABP move from a style of thinking about the future toward a full plan for action. We have found utility in stopping the process short of Step 5 as a means simply of engaging users in a different approach to dealing with the uncertainties inherent in planning.

ASSUMPTION-BASED PLANNING IN A PLANNING SYSTEM

The primary physical outputs, or products, of ABP are the signposts and the shaping and hedging actions. Monitoring the signposts and taking the near-term actions are the plan elements that best prepare an organization's operations or plans for the uncertain future. The greater that uncertainty is, the greater is the chance that one or more of the organization's assumptions will fail. For this reason, ABP is relatively more beneficial the more uncertain the times are, and it is relatively more effective the closer to the top of a planning organization hierarchy it is used. Finally, it is relatively more useful in a planning system when applied to plans (subplans) that are more mature. The more tentative or resource-unconstrained a plan is, the less likely it will be to reveal the assumptions that represent critical trade-offs—assumptions that are the main "grist" of the ABP process.

CONCLUDING REMARKS

Assumption-Based Planning is not a panacea. It does not purport to reveal truth about the uncertain future; it cannot replace creative thinking with formulaic certitude; it does not obviate critical judgments. Planning under great uncertainty will only be as good as the insight and care of the people doing that planning. What the methodology *does* is provide a systematic way of thinking about a future containing fundamental uncertainties about an organization's ends and a framework for, over time, dealing explicitly with those uncertainties.

Nothing done in the short term can "prove" the efficacy of a planning methodology; nor can the monitoring, over time, of a single instance of a plan generated by that methodology, unless there is a competing parallel plan. The more general test of a planning methodology is whether planners find it a useful tool for their planning problems. By that measure, Assumption-Based Planning has been a success. It has been used for planning in the Army doctrine and personnel communities and is being studied for use in the materiel and intelligence communities. It is being considered in the updating of the *Army Long-Range Planning System* (AR 11-32). ABP has also attracted interest outside the Army community, but only recently; therefore, its utility in that arena, while promising, remains moot at this time.

ACKNOWLEDGMENTS

This report owes its existence primarily to the insistence and encouragement of Dr. Lynn Davis. She saw the wider promise in a technique originally aimed at a narrow, specific problem and championed its generalization within and outside the Arroyo Center. Throughout its brief existence, Assumption-Based Planning has enjoyed the enthusiasm and critical attention of numerous RAND colleagues from various fields. Worth special mention are three Training and Doctrine Command (TRADOC) Research Associates: LTC Thomas Wegleitner and LTC William O'Malley, who gave thoughtfully and good-naturedly of their time to a brief but intense application of ABP to a mid-range planning problem; and their colleague, MAJ Gary Moody, who, in addition to participating in that application, has continued to play an important role as sanity check in the ongoing efforts to refine our understanding.

Several others have contributed disproportionately to this effort. The calm attention of Nanette Gantz made the programmatics of this effort almost transparent to the research team—a true blessing. An exploratory application of ABP to the Total Army benefited from the historical insights and keen observations of Benjamin Schwarz. The report itself owes a double debt to its two reviewers, Paul Bracken of Yale University and Stephen Drezner of RAND. In addition to being well established in the field of long-range planning, both are extremely busy. Their generosity in giving of their time and expertise is gratefully acknowledged and has improved both the exposition and content of this report. While the contents remain the sole responsibility of the authors, the impeccable physical presentation is almost entirely the work of the nonpareil Laurie Rennie and the understandable contents are due, in part, to the editing of Marian Branch.

Chapter One

INTRODUCTION

BACKGROUND AND OBJECTIVES

Organizational planning is always challenging and risk laden, but it becomes especially daunting in uncertain times, times of great change such as those the world is now in. In uncertain times, organizations cannot afford to plan for a single future. Their plans, instead, must be flexible and adaptable, and the organizations must have ways of recognizing when to adapt or shift plans in response to changing circumstances.

This report describes one such way, a planning tool called Assumption-Based Planning (ABP), developed by RAND for use in uncertain times. It is primarily a tool for improving the adaptability and robustness of existing plans, rather than a tool for creating plans. The use of Assumption-Based Planning can help make a plan more resistant to significant change. It can also help an organization to identify when to jettison one plan and shift to or develop another. Such concerns predominate in the planning process as change becomes more likely.

Assumption-Based Planning germinated and came to fruition in projects conducted by RAND to help the U.S. Army with a long-range planning exercise known as Army 21, the name given by the Army Training and Doctrine Command (TRADOC) to its planning process for Army doctrine in the twenty-first century, specifically, out to 30 years in the future. The primary goal of the Army 21 process is to inform the Army about changes that might be required in its operational concept in the future. ABP was developed in response to the shortcomings of the trend-based planning approach, the long-range planning method originally used for Army 21. A common method for planning, the trend-based approach tends to produce a future world (or worlds) with high descriptive plausibility and a clear transition from today's world to the projected world or worlds. Trends lose their predictive power in very uncertain futures, however, making a multiworld approach such as ABP a better approach.

While it is generally true that long-range plans deal with very uncertain futures, it is not conversely true that very uncertain times happen only in what would be considered long-range time frames. It is this fact that has made ABP an appropriate tool for a much wider audience, because the world entered a radically new and uncertain national security realm in the late 1980s, when the Soviet empire collapsed and the Cold War came to a close. The character of this new era is not yet known. As a result, organizations whose missions are associated with maintaining national security are faced with modifying or replacing existing plans in the face of widespread uncertainty, even in the short term.

Assumption-Based Planning was refined in the course of being applied several times as an adjunct to planning exercises under way in the U.S. Army. Those refinements led ABP to be divided into the following five basic steps, which are the primary topics of this report:

- Identify important assumptions underlying an organization's operations or plans.

- Identify assumption vulnerabilities within the planning horizon.

- Define signposts.

- Define shaping actions.

- Define hedging actions.

ORGANIZATION OF THIS REPORT

Chapters Two through Six provide detailed explanations of each of the five steps. Each chapter is organized similarly and contains three sections: "Essentials," "Illustrations," and "Practical Considerations." One can quickly grasp the fundamentals of ABP by reading

each "Essentials" section. Each "Illustrations" section provides examples of the methodology's applications; Army 21 is the foremost
example in these sections. Each "Practical Considerations" section
suggests "lessons learned" from those applications. Chapter Seven
discusses the ordering of the ABP steps from the standpoints of logical dependence and organizational objectives.   Chapter Eight
describes the role of ABP in a planning system. Chapter Nine pre-
sents concluding remarks. There are also two appendices. Appendix
A details the setting of time frames, or planning time horizons, in
ABP; Appendix B compares ABP with other planning methodologies
in both the public and private sectors.

Chapter Two

STEP 1: IDENTIFY IMPORTANT ASSUMPTIONS

ESSENTIALS

Assumption-Based Planning is predicated on the changing of an organization's operations or plans if its corresponding underlying assumptions about the world change. Unfortunately, an organization rarely makes explicit the assumptions that underlie its operations and plans, or refers to such assumptions explicitly or systematically in making new plans.

The first step of ABP involves identifying the important assumptions that an organization has made in determining how it does, or plans to do, business. The essentials in this step are understanding what is meant by an assumption, how and where to look for assumptions, and how to recognize assumptions that are "important" from an ABP standpoint. The output of this step is a list of important assumptions the organization is making about how it does or plans to do business.

What Is an Assumption?

We have defined an assumption as follows:

> An *assumption* is an assertion about some characteristic of the future that underlies the current operations or plans of an organization.

An assertion could be a fact or a judgment. The assertion "The sun has risen in the east for more than two centuries" would generally be recognized as a fact. The assertion "The sun will continue to rise in the east for the next two centuries" would have to be classified as a judgment (albeit a reasonably certain one). The problem comes not with assertions like these but with such assertions as "The Iraqi army has 3,304 tanks." Although this assertion has all the characteristics of a fact, it must be considered a judgment because it is based on indirect means of measurement. More problematic is an assertion such as "The Russian army will be the most significant military threat to the United States," because it can be interpreted by some clearly as a judgment, and others would argue vehemently that this is a fact. Because neither of the last two assertions is immutable, Assumption-Based Planning considers them to be assumptions regardless of the perceived status of their validity. For this reason, the validity of an assumption has been deliberately omitted from the definition.

Assumptions have been consciously defined very broadly. We intend that they may be descriptive, evaluative, predictive, or explanatory. Assumptions may also be explicit or implicit. If explicit, they may be either directed ("We have been told to assume there will be a NATO 15 years from now") or elected ("We are assuming no major nuclear exchange occurs in the planning period"). If implicit, they may be either unrecognized (as was the assumption that the United States will have at least parity in long-range weapons with any enemy in the *AirLand Battle-Future Umbrella Concept* generated in 1991) or suppressed (as is the assumption in that same document that there will be a separately constituted Army 15 years from now).

How and Where Do You Look for Assumptions?

We have said that an assumption is an assertion about the world that underlies current operations or plans. The most explicit such assertion is "The world *will* have the following characteristic, *therefore* we plan to do (or are doing) such and such." It is a clear indication of something in the plan that is in response to some characteristic of the world.

Rarely are assumptions so concisely stated (nor is it common for a connection between the world and a specific plan element to be so obvious). One case in which assumptions are stated clearly comes in the form of guidance that the organization has received from a higher organization, e.g., "You will assume for planning purposes that there will still be a NATO in 20 years." More often, the world the organization will face is described in general terms, and the plan then describes what the organization will do (or is doing). In a well-conceived plan, the connections between plan elements and the characteristics of the environment that prompted them are relatively easy to discern.

If the connections are not clear, it is a good idea to examine the plan for statements about what the organization will do, and to try to relate them to what they imply about the world. Statements that reflect choices (e.g., "We will stress offensive operations") are better candidates than those that express qualities (e.g., "We will produce the highest quality soldiers"). That is, unless an explicit trade-off is being made between a few high-quality soldiers and many mediocre soldiers, it is difficult to imagine some aspect of the world that would drive an Army to consciously produce the lowest quality soldiers. An Army that stresses offensive operations over defensive ones, however, is probably trying to take advantage of one or more characteristics of the world in doing so. It is here that one asks what assumptions are being made that cause a stress on offensive operations to be the "correct," or apt, choice for the world of the future.

Implicit assumptions are the most difficult to identify and defend. They must rely on "weight-of-evidence" arguments and usually require detailed knowledge of an organization's operations or plans. To say, for example, that the *AirLand Battle-Future Umbrella Concept* assumes that U.S. long-range weapons will be militarily effective, is likely to be controversial. To argue that assumption persuasively requires going through the "Umbrella Concept" documents and noting in what ways the concept relies on the weapons' effectiveness, how the concept could suffer if they are not, and noting the absence of discussion about what to do if they are not effective. Although the most difficult to perceive, implicit assumptions are also likely to be the most fruitful. History is replete with examples of assumptions being made implicitly (and recognized only in retrospect) that turned out to have consequences ranging from humorous ("Salt-shaker tops are always screwed on tightly") to deadly ("The enemy cannot possibly approach by that route").

We have talked about examining either current operations or plans for the assumptions that underlie them. In general, a plan for the future is a more desirable starting point than current operations, for two basic reasons. The first reason is that current operations may be overturned if one of the assumptions underlying them has been violated (is no longer viable) by recent events. Philosophically, the current operations could still be used as the basis for an ABP effort (with the violated assumptions clearly identified). Practically, however, it is difficult to get people to think about the old set of assumptions in that situation.

The second reason is that a plan is more likely to have its assumptions spelled out than are the current operations, which are often an amalgam of prior plans and ad hoc adjustments. A plan is often scrutinized for the coherence and rationality of its assumptions. In the work we did for Army 21,[1] for example, we used the concept for future doctrine as our starting point rather than then-current doctrine. That concept represented an approach for updating current, overtaken doctrine and had the added benefit of having just been developed by the doctrine community. It enabled us to ask direct questions of the developers about the assumptions they were explicitly and implicitly using in the development of the concept.

The situation we encountered in the Army 21 work was ideal: Written materials that defended the plan or concept were available and the developers of the plan present for discussion and consultation. It is common for plans to be documented, and the documents will always constitute the most direct window into the assumptions that underlie the plans. Documents are not the only available source, however, and other materials and avenues should also be utilized, including talking with people (particularly the plan's developers); consulting speeches, articles, or testimony on the plans; looking at studies that preceded the plans; and listening to what people say at meetings. Any materials that relate to the plan will be sources for amassing the weight of evidence so crucial for identifying particularly the implicit assumptions on which the plan rests. The

---

[1]The full details of the Army 21 work are documented in Dewar, J. A., and M. Levin, *Assumption-Based Planning for Army 21*, Santa Monica, Calif.: RAND, R-4172-A, 1992.

same, of course, holds true if the current operations are being used instead of a formal plan.

How Do You Identify Important Assumptions?

As defined, assumptions an organization is making are easy to identify. The definition we have chosen is general, allowing, for example, a wide variety of obvious, physical facts to qualify as assumptions for *any* organization. Many facts about nominal human characteristics, physical laws, geographical "constants" (e.g., tectonic plates) implicitly underlie any organizational plan. In ABP we care only about important assumptions:

> An assumption is *important* if its negation would lead to significant changes in the current operations or plans of an organization.

This is not the usual connotation of *important*. In Army 21, for example, one of the assumptions underlying the future concept was "The Army will fight combined with the forces of other nations." If the Army does not fight combined in some instance, its current operations remain unchanged, and from an ABP standpoint, the assumption is not important. Which is not to say that fighting combined is not important; indeed, the Army has spent a great deal of energy and money to prepare itself for fighting combined. Rather, we emphasize that the assumption is not sensitive to *whether* we fight combined. On the other hand, another assumption underlying the future concept was "Our long-range weapons will be militarily effective." If they are not, the concept is seriously undermined. Therefore, "Our long-range weapons will be militarily effective" is an *important assumption*.

ILLUSTRATIONS

Army 21[2]

Our first decision in the Army 21 work concerned where to look for assumptions. Army 21 is part of a larger effort that encompasses cur-

---

[2]Again, see Dewar and Levin, 1992.

rent Army doctrine (as codified in *Field Manual [FM] 100-5)* and *AirLand Battle-Future* (which looks at doctrine out to 15 years in the future). The current Army operational concept is "AirLand Battle" (as codified primarily in *TRADOC Pamphlet 525-5* [dated 1981], *FM 100-5* [dated 1986], and supporting documents). However, *FM 100-5* is scheduled to be revised, and, at the time of the Army 21 work, that revision was expected to be based on the *AirLand Battle-Future (ALB-F) Umbrella Concept* (dated September 1990), developed at the Combined Arms Center. The revision of *FM 100-5* is intended to update the Army's operational concept and bring it into consonance with the dramatic changes occurring in the former Soviet Union and Eastern Europe, as well as with the war in the Persian Gulf. The AirLand Battle-Future Umbrella Concept was still in draft form and was being evaluated throughout the Army.

Assumption-Based Planning for Army 21 depended on identifying the assumptions about the world that underlay the Army's operational concept. Therefore, it was inappropriate to use the assumptions underlying *FM 100-5*, but it is also somewhat premature to use those underlying the *AirLand Battle-Future Umbrella Concept*. For our purposes, we chose the latter document because of its coherence, and we chose September 1990 as a specific cutoff date. Since then, the operational concept had its name changed to AirLand Operations (ALO) and is undergoing further revision. Nonetheless, we chose that document as the starting point of our planning work and collected the relevant documents published on or before September 1990.

Those documents were the final output of the development team at the Combined Arms Center at Fort Leavenworth, Kansas. They represent a convenient hiatus in the development process, and we were able to interview members of the development team about assumptions at a point when their work was in stasis. We read the documents and gleaned as many explicit and implicit assumptions as possible—about two dozen, with slightly over half being explicitly called out in the "AirLand Battle-Future" documentation.

In discussions with the framers of ALB-F, we arrived at a consensus list of 23 assumptions that underlay ALB-F. In the final list, 15 were explicit assumptions and eight were implicit assumptions. Table 2.1

Table 2.1

Sample Assumptions Underlying ALB-F Umbrella Concept

Explicit
• The Army will conduct joint operations (with other services).
• Some potential enemies will have significant quantities of high-quality weapons (including those of mass destruction) as sophisticated as our own or more so.
• The Army will not be heavily forward-deployed in conflict arenas of greatest concern.
• We will prefer nonlinear operations because they take advantage of our relative strengths.
• Battlefields will be nonlinear, with unavoidable intermingling of opposing forces.

Implicit
• The enemy may come from anywhere, but is more likely to come from the lesser developed countries.
• We will have at least rough parity in surveillance assets, long-range weapons, and mobility.
• Our long-range weapons will be militarily effective.
• The Army will continue to play a primary role in maintaining global stability across the operational continuum.

shows examples of both explicit and implicit assumptions from that list.

All the 23 assumptions we identified were not necessarily important. In retrospect, of the examples in Table 2.1, only the implicit assumptions are arguably important according to our definition. All, however, pass the qualifications of an assumption as laid out earlier.

Our primary goal in reading the ALB-F documents and talking with the developers was to understand as much as possible about the world for which the ALB-F operational concept was developed. The primary assumptions made in developing the ALB-F concept are about matters of concern to the Army and its missions. Consequently, some of the assumptions are about how the Army will react and behave, which are of interest in other contexts. The assumptions about the world that the Army had little or no control over are what mainly interest us.

In this regard, it is important to make a distinction between whether the *assumptions* underlying Army doctrine are relevant and whether the *doctrine* itself is. That is, it is one thing to correctly intuit the nature of the global security environment (assumptions) and another to correctly decide what to do about it (doctrine). The assumptions we tried to identify, then, are those about the world over which the Army has little or no control and upon which the appropriateness of the AirLand Battle-Future Umbrella Concept depends.

PRACTICAL CONSIDERATIONS

Too Many Assumptions

Identifying assumptions well requires a good deal of judgment and creativity, because some of the important assumptions an organization makes are obvious; others are very subtle and hidden; and still others are only marginally important or are clearly important but clearly invulnerable. Limits must be set at some point. For example, in answer to How many important assumptions can one be expected to find in a given organization? it is conceivable that in this step too many important assumptions can be identified. There are no hard rules here about how many is too many, but 2,000 is clearly too many; thus, it *may* be necessary to curtail, or winnow, the list before proceeding to the next step.

The decision of which assumptions to keep must be made on the basis of importance: If the list is completed and deemed too long or if the list is under way and endless, the definition of *important* should be tightened and the less-important assumptions deleted. More specifically, the magnitude of the organizational changes required by a negated assumption should be mentally increased before an assumption is considered important. To prevent the loss of important assumptions in such a winnowing process, senior officials can help identify the truly key assumptions that should be carried on in the ABP process.

Two important caveats must be made here with regard to reducing the number of assumptions. First, to avoid prejudging how many assumptions should eventually be analyzed in detail, the list of important assumptions should be winnowed only under extreme circumstances. That is, err on the side of inclusion and at least wait until Step 2 to see if what looks like an inordinate number gets reduced down in the more natural process of identifying assumptions that are vulnerable within the time horizon. Most important is to encourage the identification of those judgments about the world that have been ossified into "facts" in an organization's thinking, for it is surely these that promise the greatest chance for serious disruption in the organization's future.

The second caveat concerns division of responsibility. Implicit in Assumption-Based Planning is a division of responsibility between planners and leaders. Generally, the planners identify all possible changes that could threaten the plans of an organization and recommend actions that the organization should take in light of those possible changes. They are responsible for avoiding planning failures—or failures to identify "foreseeable" events—that could affect the organization's plans and goals. It is the responsibility of leadership (among others) to ensure that the planning process is timely and efficient and, ultimately, to decide which of the planner-identified actions to incorporate into the plan.

With this division of responsibility, any time a decision is made that reduces the number of planners' legitimate options (such as leaving some important assumptions off the assumption list), it should be made either by, or in concert with, leadership, or with the explicit authority of leadership.

How Do You Identify All the Assumptions?

Assumption-Based Planning is predicated on identifying all an organization's important assumptions. Although it is clearly not possible to know when you have them all, the more thorough and thoughtful the planners are, the more important assumptions they are likely to identify. Repeated applications of the ABP process improve the chances that all the important assumptions an organization is making will be identified.

Once an important assumption is identified and listed, it remains an important assumption (unless overtaken by events) for the next planning cycle. The list of important assumptions will thus tend to get longer with each succeeding planning cycle. Over time, then,

through repeated applications of ABP the assumptions an organization is making will be more comprehensively identified.

In any event, the problem of missing potentially important assumptions in one planning cycle is not nearly as important as focusing on
the most important of the identified assumptions and spending time
on them. In this way, over time, one can reasonably expect that the
truly crucial assumptions an organization is making will be examined
and evaluated.

Important Assumptions and Politics

So far this chapter has been written as though all planning decisions
will ultimately be based either on professional expertise or on position in the organization. There is a third possibility that falls under
the general rubric of "politics."[3] For better or worse, *politics*—the
give and take of institutional compromise—both internal to an
organization and outside it, is likely to affect planning decisions.
Politics, in this sense, is a part of any organizational decisions and
may well appear in the review of any list of important assumptions.
How should ABP handle this?

Politics can be thought of as a particular view of which assumptions
are important and which are not, there being no *absolute* measure of
the importance of assumptions. By trying to identify "apolitically" as
many of the important assumptions as possible, ABP makes more
explicit where and how politics enters into the planning process and
offers a channel for responsible dissenters, critics, and skeptics to
make their case and not be stifled by narrow professionalism or bu-
reaucratic forces. Politics is not necessarily an evil influence. In the
1920s, for example, the Army bureaucracy clamped down on the
further study of tank warfare, and only the political skill on the part
of some officers kept the study of tank operations alive.

We have talked about identifying even suppressed assumptions. ABP
is "agnostic" on whether it is best for those assumptions to remain

---

[3]The authors are indebted to Paul Bracken of Yale University for much of this discussion.

suppressed, but emphasizes the utility of reviewing even the suppressed assumptions, on occasion (even if it must be done in private), for their importance and vulnerability.

Chapter Three

STEP 2: IDENTIFY ASSUMPTION VULNERABILITIES

ESSENTIALS

Step 2 consists of testing the organization's important assumptions, identified in Step 1, against what could happen in the future in order to identify those assumptions that are vulnerable. An assumption is *vulnerable* if a plausible event in the world would cause it to fail (no longer be viable) within the *planning time horizon*, the farthest point out the planning will consider. This chapter describes the role of the planning time horizon in identifying vulnerabilities, the process of determining what might happen in the future, and criteria for assessing vulnerability.

The Planning Time Horizon

An organization's assumptions are time dependent. That is, they are not immutable facts but rather are projected to hold true for a certain period of time. An assumption's likelihood of being negated, its vulnerability to change at some point in the future, depends on the length of time to that point, or the planning time horizon. Without a planning time horizon, *every* assumption is vulnerable. With the horizon, only those assumptions that could plausibly change within that horizon are vulnerable. A planning time horizon is thus a crucial component in Assumption-Based Planning.

For some planning efforts, the time horizon will have been set by a higher level in the planning organization. For other efforts, the organization will be called upon to set its own horizon. From a methodological standpoint, the only restriction on the planning time horizon is that it be in the future.

From a more practical standpoint, how the planning time horizon is set is a matter of great importance to the planning system: It is a complex function of the planning environment, the organization's missions, and the intent of the planning. Details of selecting a planning time horizon are discussed in Appendix A. Assumption-Based Planning requires only that the planning time horizon has been established.

Identifying Elements of Change

To determine which assumptions may be vulnerable within the planning horizon, a strong sense of what the world *could* be like at that horizon is necessary. Much of futures research is focused on what can be said with reasonable certainty about the future—what *will* happen. The intent in ABP is not to predict the world at the planning horizon, but to identify the broader set of events that could plausibly happen within the horizon. To make clear this distinction, we refer to those events that could plausibly happen within the horizon as elements of change. Formally, an *element of change* is an event or world condition that satisfies three conditions:

1.   represents change from today;

2.   is plausible within the planning time horizon; and

3.   is related to the organization and its plans.

Of these three, the first condition is trivial (but necessary). The second and third conditions obviously require a good deal of judgment. The second requires care to avoid the failure common to the technological community (and others) of underestimating how quickly change *can* (as opposed to *will*) occur. The third condition requires judgment and care to avoid failures of the type that affected the Swiss watchmaking community, who produced the first digital watch but decided it was a curiosity and not really related to their profession. Because of that community's shortsightedness, the Japanese have come to dominate the watch market as the Swiss once did.

Philosophically, Assumption-Based Planning is unconcerned with *how* elements of change are identified. Any method for generating plausible ideas about the changes that could take place out to the planning horizon is useful: trend extrapolations (not used for predicting), expert opinion, historical analogs, simulations, "gut" feelings, gaming, for example. Some can be argued to work better than others, but any combination of methods that produces a robust set of elements of change out to the planning horizon is acceptable.

Identifying Vulnerabilities

What makes an assumption vulnerable are those elements of change that, were they to come about, would violate the assumption or cause it to be wrong. In general, an assumption may be subject to violation in more than one way. For example, in the past an important assumption for the Army's operational concept was that the Army was heavily forward-deployed in Europe. There were various ways, over time, that the Army could have found itself not heavily forward-deployed in Europe: The threat could have disappeared (as has happened), Europe could have been overrun, the Europeans could have asked the Army to leave, public opinion in the United States could have forced the president to call for troop withdrawal, and the United States could have disbanded its army. At any given planning horizon, these specific changes were more or less plausible. As a rule of thumb, *any* plausible change in the world that would cause an assumption to fail within the planning time horizon is sufficient to identify that assumption as vulnerable.

In the above example, having the threat disappear would not have been identified as the most plausible change, or assumption violation. Given the number of plausible future changes, it is common to assign notional or even numerical probabilities to the likelihood of such changes. However, the most important goal of Step 2 should be to identify as many of the important assumptions as possible that are vulnerable to changes within the planning time horizon and to capture the ways in which they are vulnerable, as the following examples illustrate.

ILLUSTRATIONS

Army 21

Identifying the vulnerable assumptions in Army 21 was a two-step process. The first step identified plausible elements of change in the world that could occur during the next 25 to 30 years and that could affect the Army's operational concept. We relied on a structured form of gathering expert opinion—the Delphi process—to collect this information. The second step matched the elements of change with the assumptions from Step 1 of ABP to identify the vulnerable assumptions.

The Delphi methodology, originally conceived at RAND as a means of eliciting group opinion without the influence of a dominant member of the group, has a long and varied history.[1] Although typically used to develop consensus among experts, Delphis have also been used heuristically to help explore a topic more completely than might be possible with input from only one or two people. It is in this heuristic mode that we used the Delphi process for Army 21.

In developing the question that served as the starting point for our Delphi experiment, we were concerned with breaking the lock that trend extrapolation typically has on long-range military planning (see Appendix B). As a means of minimizing the natural tendency to extrapolate from current events, we placed a high premium in the Delphi on denying the participants, Army and RAND experts, information about world events leading up to the time period in question. Our hope was that that denial would help focus participant attention on longer term issues critical to military planning.

To move the participants in that direction, we established the following artificial situation:

> You have been asleep for the last 30 years. You know nothing about the world at this point except that there has been no major nuclear war in the intervening years. You are asked to guess what the Army's roles, missions, and operational concept are [presuming they are well

---

[1]See Dalkey, Norman C., *The Delphi Method: An Experimental Study of Group Opinion*, Santa Monica, Calif.: RAND, RM-5888-PR, June 1968, and Sackman, Harold, *Delphi Critique*, Lexington, Mass.: Lexington Books, 1975, p. 1.

suited to the new world]. Before you answer, you may ask 10 questions about today's world. Each question must have a yes or no answer, and none can be contingent on a previous question.

What is your list of questions?

By denying the participants knowledge of the world for 30 years, we hoped to focus them, as much as possible, on long-range issues relevant to the Army concept. By restricting them to questions with yes or no answers, we hoped to focus their attention on concrete aspects of the future.

We conducted the Delphi in three rounds. In the first round each participant was asked to develop his list of questions independently. In the second round, the entire list of questions generated by all the participants was circulated and each participant was asked to reconsider the questions in light of the questions others had asked, then pose a new set of questions (10 per participant). In the final round, each person was sent his list of questions from the second round and asked both to rank them and to explain the connection between his questions and changes in the Army operational concept.

As with any attempt to capture expert opinion, a Delphi is only as broad and comprehensive as the sample of experts queried. Although our sample size was both relatively small (16 people began the experiment; 14 completed the third round) and institutionally limited (all respondents were at RAND, but almost half were active-duty officers assigned to RAND in the Army Fellows Program), we were confident that we captured much of the relevant expertise desired. Our sample included senior national security analysts with knowledge of regional issues, strategic matters, technology, manpower, and defense planning, and experience in the State Department, Office of the Secretary of Defense, Congressional Budget Office, and the services. The Army Fellows represented the combat arms, combat support arms, and combat service support branches; and they had a broad range of experience, from field duty through high-level staff assignments.

By structuring the Delphi as we did, the questions yielded plausible elements of change 25–30 years in the future that are related to the Army and its operational concept. Specifically, they satisfy the three required characteristics of elements of change:

- First, the questions *did* speak to change. To state what perhaps is obvious, respondents would not have asked questions were they not concerned about potential, impending change. (No one, for example, asked if the sun still came up in the morning or if the seas still contained water.)

- Second, the elements of change had plausibility within the 25–30-year time frame. The concern of the experts about the changes gave the changes plausibility, and the Delphi process itself worked toward a sanity check on that plausibility.

- Third, the questions were directly related to the Army and its operational concept. This focus on the Army's concept is what facilitated looking for specific elements of change that violated specific assumptions.

Identifying elements of change that violate important assumptions is a demanding, "think hard," part of the assumption-based methodology. We have not yet developed an explicit, systematic procedure for performing this synthesizing task. There are various ways to make the search for such violated-assumption–element-of-change pairs, but little more rigor than that can be brought to what must, at this point, be a creative process.

In the example here, the process of identifying potential violated-assumption–element-of-change pairs was done in discussion sessions with the group that had administered the Delphi and the group that participated in the assumption-identification process. The resulting inevitable biases are, we think, ameliorated both by having discussed the assumptions with the framers of the operational concept and by collecting the wisdom of more than a dozen colleagues on the elements of change. Four assumption–element pairs, shown in Table 3.1, were identified to be carried forward for expansion into full-blown future worlds. The elements of change are shown in the form of the question asked as part of the Delphi. In each case, there is a secondary element of change, or question, that helped focus the specific alternative future with its assumption–element pair.

Table 3.1

Assumption–Element-of-Change Pairs

Assumption	Element of Change
The Army will continue to play a primary role in maintaining global stability across the operational continuum.	Is the United States still maintaining the role of world policeman, either unilaterally or predominantly? [Has the United Nations become a cohesive body with sufficient military capability to enforce sanctions?]
The United States will have at least rough parity in surveillance assets, long-range weapons, and mobility.	Is there a nation with a military force that could be construed as a threat to the United States or its national policy? [Is there a competitive military superpower, like the Soviet Union/Russian Republic (or rearmed Japan or emergent Brazil) which can destroy the United States?]
The predominance of Army operations will be covered by ALB-F.	Did the Army take on more domestic [missions] . . .? [Are there any severe threats to the global environment that could lead to U.S. intervention for protection of the environment?]
Our long-range systems will be militarily effective.	Have there been substantial breakthroughs in weapons, propulsion, and transportation technologies? [Are projectile weapons still the predominant force on the battlefield?]

PRACTICAL CONSIDERATIONS

This step identifies those important assumptions that are vulnerable within the planning time horizon. Each vulnerable assumption is associated with one or more distinct ways in which it could be violated. This step, too, could produce too many assumption–vulnerability pairs by carrying over too many important assumptions from Step 1 and/or by identifying too many distinct vulnerabilities per assumption.

Again, judgment will be required to establish how many vulnerable assumptions are too many. But if it *is* deemed necessary to winnow the list of assumption–vulnerability pairs, risk should be the criterion. *Risk,* roughly, is the product of the importance (as identified in Step 1) and the probability of the assumption's failing within the time horizon. Therefore, if the list is too long or is getting too long, the notion of the risk associated with each assumption–vulnerability pair should be used to winnow the list by deleting the least-risky assumption–vulnerability pairs from further consideration.

Again, winnowing should be resisted at this stage to preclude pre-judging which vulnerable assumptions will eventually be analyzed in detail.   The once-perceived unlikelihood of removal of threat in Europe is an example of a winnowing candidate that came to pass. Again, winnowing should be done in explicit concert with organizational leadership.

The Delphi used in Army 21 has some advantages in identifying elements of change.   But there are other ways of identifying those elements. The most important consideration in generating the elements of change is to ensure that concentration is on what *could* happen, not on what *will* happen. A common tendency among analysts considering the future is to try to predict what will happen. Great vigilance and concentration are required instead to deal with the breadth of future possibilities rather than trying to refine them down to one's own best guess.

The greater the breadth of knowledge base included in this process, the more effective the ABP process will be. Similarly, the more open the minds gathered to work this part of the problem, the better. It is neither required nor necessarily a boon for minds—idea sources—to have specific knowledge of the organization. In the step of identifying the organization's assumptions, knowledge of the organization was crucial, but here it is almost better to have people outside the organization identifying changes that could take place within the planning time horizon.

We have set forth the identification of vulnerability causes and of vulnerable assumptions as though they were necessarily separate enterprises. There is much to be said both for using the assumptions to help identify vulnerability causes and for using the vulnerability causes to help identify other assumptions—particularly implicit ones.

Chapter Four

STEP 3: DEFINE SIGNPOSTS

ESSENTIALS

Assumption-Based Planning is driven by the notion that the best approach in an uncertain planning environment is to do what needs doing *now* and to watch out for changes that will resolve the uncertainties in the future. To this point, the ABP process has produced a collection of important assumptions along with their vulnerabilities. Steps 4 and 5 of ABP deal with what actions an organization should take now to best deal with the vulnerability of those assumptions (and therefore of the plan). Even if no actions were necessary beyond those already in the plan, it is important to be alert for evidence that assumptions underlying that plan are becoming vulnerable, or are changing. Signposts are the mechanism for doing that and are the products of this step.

Signposts are indicators, or warning signals, that the vulnerability of an assumption may be changing; specifically,

> a *signpost* is an event or threshold that clearly indicates the changing vulnerability of an assumption.

Establishing signposts is not necessarily an easy task. The most difficult criterion in the definition is that the signpost be a clear indication. At the least, this criterion demands that the indication be both unambiguous and genuine. Of the two conditions, the unambiguous indication is likely to be the more difficult to ensure. For example, one of the Army 21 worlds had the United Nations taking over the role of world's policeman from the United States. One indication of the takeover would be that the U.N. stepped in to bring about peace in some incipient conflict. On one hand, there would be no reason to misrepresent this indication. It is genuine. On the other hand, a single instance of taking over the role may not constitute a clear, confirming indication that the United Nations was, indeed, becoming the world's policeman; nor would U.N. intervention in all seven of the next incipient conflicts, nor in three of the next four conflicts, be unambiguous. In this case, any time the U.N. steps into an incipient conflict instead of the United States, it should be taken as a corroborating instance of the increasing vulnerability of the assumption; conversely, there can be countervailing instances. Some judgment is necessary to decide what collections of corroborating and countervailing instances will constitute a *clear indication* about the movement of an assumption's vulnerability.

In setting up signposts, misrepresentation is a serious concern. It is not difficult to imagine indications that are deceiving: a military opponent sending false messages, a bank robber brandishing an unloaded gun, a potential buyer insisting that his or her offer is final. Signposts that are difficult to misrepresent are clearly preferable, although not always possible.

Signposts are assumption specific, but a single signpost may portend the violation of more than one assumption. In 1985, indications that the Soviet Union was about to break up would have affected the solidity of assumptions underlying everything from nuclear deterrence to basing strategies, to containment strategies, to the future of the North Atlantic Treaty Organization (NATO).

A given assumption is likely to require several signposts, either to increase the likelihood of detecting an emerging threat or to monitor several ways in which an assumption might be threatened. Signposts are typically thought of as being things to monitor *today*; however, the notion of defining signposts whose monitoring is contingent on the triggering of some other signpost should not be precluded.

Along with identifying signposts, the planners should establish at least a preliminary monitoring concept, because some signposts may require monitoring by those outside the planners' organization. In the military, for example, signposts pertinent to assumptions about foreign technology affect the doctrine community but are often more appropriately monitored by the intelligence community or the technology community.

ILLUSTRATIONS

Army 21

For Army 21, TRADOC sponsored a workshop at which four separate worlds were developed and investigated. Each world was developed by assuming that one of the vulnerable assumptions (from Step 2) had actually been violated and then describing both how it changed and what some of the consequences were. We see the developing of such worlds as more specifically important for defining hedging actions (see Chapter Six), but defining signposts through these worlds posed no problem.

Defining the signposts was different for the different kinds of worlds. Two of the worlds were technological in orientation and two were political. On the technological side, a good example is the world in which the military effectiveness of our long-range weapons was negated through weapons proliferation. In this world, the signposts were technology oriented and relatively unequivocal because visible evidence of this type of proliferation is available: technology demonstrations, system fieldings, and clear proliferation of counterprecision and/or counterstealth technology. Further, there are relatively clear requirements on the time it takes between a technology demonstration and system fielding, providing an approximate schedule for the assumption's degradation.

Such technology signposts are common and relatively well known in the materiel and acquisition communities. Although they are subject to misrepresentation, they are reasonably unambiguous and relatively predictable. Another type of signpost identified for this world was the occurrence of a conflict in which it was clear that our long-range weapons systems were ineffective. The element of surprise—such as the anti-tank weapons in the 1973 Arab-Israeli War—confounds the warning signs that this assumption is changing and argues for hedging actions of some type to be taken immediately.

In one of the political worlds, a different difficulty arose in trying to define signposts that were clear. In the world in which the Army no longer continues to play a primary role in maintaining global stability across the operational continuum, the indications of change are much more equivocal. The workshop focused on two aspects of change in that world. The first was the emergence of the United Nations as the primary international peacekeeping organization, as discussed in "Essentials" of this chapter. Recent deployment of U.N. troops in Croatia would be seen as a further indication of the emergence of the United Nations as a peacekeeper; but it is an equivocal indicator in the sense that this application has to do with an intranational struggle. Indicators of this type are difficult to misrepresent, but are much less likely to be seen as clear evidence that a particular assumption is no longer viable.

The workshop also identified indicators pertaining to the U.S. domestic situation—a seriously worsening economy, violent domestic unrest, a national service debate—that would strengthen assumptions that the Army might be turning away from the international arena to concentrate on internal matters. However, despite concerted effort, no single incident was identified that would *clearly signal* the arrival of this world. The example that follows indicates that incidents of this type *are* sometimes available.

Royal Dutch/Shell

In his book on strategic planning, Peter Schwartz describes the role of signposts in Royal Dutch/Shell's corporate plans.[1] In one plan, Shell was contemplating building a large, multibillion-dollar platform to take natural gas from the Troll gas field in the North Atlantic. Among the assumptions underlying the rationale for the platform, one was that the price of natural gas would stay at levels it had enjoyed for nearly 10 years. Shell was worried, however, that if political relations between the then–Soviet Union and NATO nations changed for the better, the Europeans could drop their informal agreement that no more than 35 percent of their gas and oil markets would be open to the Soviet Union. This change would open the doors for

---

[1]Schwartz, Peter, *The Art of the Long View*, New York: Doubleday Currency, May 1991, pp. 47–60.

cheap gas and oil from the Soviet Union and prices could drop precipitously. Signposts Shell needed to monitor would be associated with thawing of relations between the Soviets and NATO nations.

Shell planners reckoned that any loosening of political control in the Soviet Union would require a justification akin to the "New Economic Policy" Lenin used in 1920 to combat massive unrest over food rationing. (That policy lasted seven years, until Stalin ended it.) So Shell set up, in its parlance, a *scenario*, called the "Greening of Russia," in which the Soviet Union underwent massive economic and political restructuring, including a significant opening up to the West and a cessation of the 35-percent limit.

Shell planners then identified several potential leaders of such a new movement, including Mikhail Gorbachev. They also looked for Russian economists who might be leaders of such a movement and identified, among others, Abel Agenbegyan. In 1985, Gorbachev brought Agenbegyan to Moscow as his chief economic adviser; together, they loosened up centralized control in grand, historic fashion. It now looks, indeed, as though the 35-percent limit will fall.

Shell planners had worked through the actions for responding to the "Greening of Russia" scenario, and, although Schwartz gives no specific details, we are left to presume that Shell followed the basic actions identified. Shell *did* take some actions as a result merely of the plausibility of this scenario. Those actions are discussed in the "Illustrations" of Chapter Six.

Book Publishing

In discussing the planning for a book publisher, Schwartz mentions signposts for recognizing an increase in general book readership (a rise in childhood literacy rates; a number of new bookstores opening up and surviving for three years; the appearance of high-level serious books in, say, airport bookstores) or a decrease (a drop in literacy rates; a rise in picture books or books about television; a decline in independent bookstores, especially in suburban areas).

PRACTICAL CONSIDERATIONS

Signposts are tied to a vulnerable assumption. A practical consideration in achieving the goal of defining how the assumption might be violated is to ignore signposts about aspects of the world irrelevant to the violation of the assumption. For example, consider a world in which the Army finds itself spending most of its time cleaning up environmental disasters instead of training for war, which violates the assumption that the Army is primarily a warfighting organization. The world used to explore this violated assumption might contain a detailed nuclear accident the Army is called on to help contain and clean up. Signposts that would be of interest to a nuclear engineer for foreseeing the nuclear accident are largely irrelevant for exploring the Army in a toxic-cleanup world. It is sufficient to know that the probability of a nuclear accident is high enough to make such an accident a plausible occurrence and one that could require Army assistance.

Another practical consideration with signposts regards who should do the monitoring. Not all the signposts are best monitored by the same organization as that doing the planning. The planners should also try to identify proper monitoring agencies for the signposts and ensure that the monitoring is feasible.

Chapter Five

STEP 4: DEFINE SHAPING ACTIONS

ESSENTIALS

Typically, an organization has made major investments based on the solidity of its important assumptions. This implies both that it will generally view the vulnerability of any assumption negatively and that it will do little projecting of consequences to substantiate that view. At issue is what action the organization can and should take to control or shape the situation so that an important assumption does not (or does, depending on the view) fail.

To the extent that the organization can control the situation, it can define and take actions to encourage or avert the changing of an important assumption. Such actions are shaping actions, and they depend primarily on the vulnerability of an assumption and the plausible mechanisms that cause the vulnerability. Specifically,

> a *shaping action* is an organizational action to be taken in the current planning cycle and is intended to control the vulnerability of an important assumption.

Shaping actions are a common part of everyday life. They are codified in such maxims as "An ounce of prevention is worth a pound of cure." Actions that shape the future are not viewed so much as preventive as success oriented, a view that is ingrained in American private industry: "The organization knows what it wants and will move mountains [definitely a shaping action] to get it."

Unlike private industry, the military is generally thought to be more reactive to, than controlling of, the nation's interests and wishes. However, the services have considerable autonomy within broadly defined national-security strategies and can control a variety of factors that shape their future. An army that has a technological advantage in materiel, for example, routinely engages in shaping actions designed to prevent its materiel advantages from being negated or superseded by an enemy. Similarly, a service that assumes a certain level of funding in its planning will take shaping actions in the halls of Congress during budgeting cycles to try to ensure that funding level.

We have emphasized averting the changing or violation of an important assumption. But the definition of shaping actions also encompasses actions intended to cause such violations. But how is it that one might want an important assumption to fail? As a trivial example, consider a tactical military plan predicated on the enemy's using a specific avenue of approach. The planners then contemplate a second enemy avenue of approach. They develop a plan that makes using the second avenue of approach much worse for the enemy. At this point the planners might actually prefer that the enemy not use the assumed first avenue of approach, and would want to take action designed to make the second avenue appear more attractive to the enemy.

To clarify the definition, then, shaping actions work either to prevent an assumption-threatening world from occurring or to steer events toward a preferred world. They are, in a sense, independent of contemplation of that potential world.

ILLUSTRATIONS

Army 21

In the TRADOC-sponsored workshop described in Chapter Four, after fleshing out the details and implications of its world, each group came to a consensus on whether that world was a desirable world from the Army standpoint. Surprisingly, because any change is generally resisted, arriving at a consensus was not always easy. Once desirability was decided, the shaping actions could be identified. As with signposts, the type of world made a marked difference in the ease of defining shaping actions.

In the world in which the Army no longer continues to play a primary role in maintaining global stability across the operational continuum, shaping actions were difficult to define: Little in that world is under the direct control of the Army. In the more technological world, a world in which the effectiveness of U.S. long-range weapons systems is negated, it was much easier to define shaping actions. This latter is not a world of the Army's liking.

The single most important shaping action to avoid such a world is to concentrate research and development (R&D) efforts on maintaining the effectiveness of U.S. long-range weapons systems. This shaping action specifically implies spending "enough" money in the technology base on countermeasures and counter-countermeasures to the technologies responsible for the U.S. edge in long-range weapons systems—precision guidance and stealth. Although this action may appear somewhat obvious, the ABP process points out the particular importance of such an R&D emphasis and links the vulnerability of the Army's doctrine to any erosion in its technology edge in this area.

Royal Dutch/Shell

An interesting example of a shaping action comes, again, from Royal Dutch/Shell. One of the assumptions Shell planners tested was that oil prices would remain at high levels. They looked at specific ways oil prices could collapse (and developed hedging actions as discussed in the next chapter). Shell recognized that a price collapse would affect all oil companies relatively equally and that Shell would be forced to sell its gasoline for less unless it could find a unique way to enhance the gas. Shell identified a shaping action to keep gas prices high: It began research on an environmentally clean, high-performance gasoline, with the intention of selling it more profitably at a higher price.

PRACTICAL CONSIDERATIONS

The shaping actions defined in Step 4 are intended as responses to an assumption the organization is making today about the future, an assumption that has not yet been violated. And there is no guarantee that the assumption will be violated. Given this fundamental uncertainty in when or whether the assumption will fail, a serious question is, When should the actions be taken, if at all? Taking all the planner-generated actions now is not necessarily an incorrect response, but it is generally an impractical one.

It is important, then, to identify those actions that *should* be taken in the near term (or within this planning cycle[1]) to prepare for the potential violation of assumptions. And although that identification is ultimately a leadership responsibility, reducing the number of actions that should be considered for implementation in the near term is the important role of the planner.

To identify whether an action should be considered in the near term, the planner should answer three questions about the action and its associated assumption:

1. How soon may the assumption fail?

2. How well can the violation be foreseen?

3. How much time will be required for an action associated with the violation to be realized?

The answers require significant judgment by experts. The first question is to ascertain the earliest that the assumption may plausibly become invalid. The second question relates to the signposts from the previous step (Step 3), which seeks indicators that this particular assumption is failing. The final question deals with the time it will nominally take before the effects of the action can have the desired outcome.

Once the answers are achieved, however, the planner can decide quickly whether an action should be taken in the near term by the two-question logical computation represented in Figure 5.1. The first question, essentially question 2 above, is whether there will be

---

[1]In the Army planning system, near-term actions affect Army plans no closer than two years out. Planning does not affect the budget that extends two years into the future; therefore, the closest action to today would be programming money into the system for two years in the future.

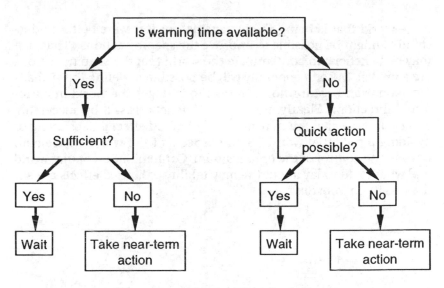

Figure 5.1—Warning-Time Logic Tree

warning that an assumption is failing. If the answer is yes, then warning is available, and the next question is whether that warning is sufficient. That is, Is the warning likely to be enough in advance to provide the time required for the action to be realized (question 3 above)? If yes, then the actions can wait at least until the warning is triggered. If no, then it is not safe to wait for warning and that action should be considered for near-term implementation.

If the answer to the warning availability question is no, the second question in this logic system is whether the action can be accomplished quickly enough to be of benefit after it is clear that the assumption has failed. That is, Can the action be implemented quickly? If yes, then again it is safe to wait until the assumption breaks. If no, that action should be considered for near-term implementation.

The outputs of this computation are two sets of shaping actions: A set of shaping actions that should be considered for near-term implementation and a set of shaping actions that may become important in the future if their associated assumptions ever fail.

If the world that is being shaped against (or for) were better understood, it might be possible to improve the shaping actions. That is, it may be beneficial to contemplate the world that the shaping actions are aimed at. Also, it generally will be possible to define those shaping actions an organization can take to "nudge" the world in a preferred direction. Clearly, not all shaping actions will be successful, and even those that are may have only limited effect on achieving or avoiding a potential world. Some aspects of the world will remain beyond the control of the organization. Contemplation of that world and what to do today about the inevitability of limited effects are addressed in Chapter Six.

STEP 5: DEFINE HEDGING ACTIONS

ESSENTIALS

Signposts are sought to monitor changes in the world, and shaping actions are taken to change the world in ways desirable to the organization. But what should the organization do if the world, despite the organization's best efforts, changes in ways inimical to the current plan? The answer is, "Take hedging actions." Defining hedging actions is the final step of ABP.

Hedging Actions

Hedging actions are those actions that enable the organization to cope with a world beyond its control. More specifically,

> *a hedging action* is an organizational action to be taken in the current planning cycle and is intended to better prepare an organization for the failure of one of its important assumptions.

If defining shaping actions is the success-oriented part of ABP, defining hedging actions is the failure-oriented part. Hedging actions necessarily derive from and depend on the vulnerability of a particular assumption. Unlike shaping actions, hedging actions do not reflect an opinion about the particular world. They are actions that should be taken regardless of the desirability of the world, to ensure that the organization will be prepared if that world eventuates.

Making backup plans to move a picnic indoors in case of rain should be done regardless of whether you are looking forward to the picnic in the first place. The possibility of rain is sufficient impetus to develop the hedging actions. Hedging actions are those that should be done now, before it begins to rain: clearing a space indoors for the table and chairs; assigning people to carry parts of the picnic indoors if it starts raining; and moving the barbecue under the eaves so that rain will not hit the hotdogs once barbecuing commences. None of these actions keeps the rain from falling, but they all better prepare the picnic organizers to save the picnic in case it does rain. Many further tasks will be required when, and if, the rain starts falling (such as actually carrying the table and chairs indoors), but they do not need to be done before rainfall or some further indication of its imminence.

Defining hedging actions for a given vulnerable assumption requires visualizing the situation in which the assumption is violated: a rain shower in the picnic example. Defining shaping actions does not necessarily require such visualization. In the picnic example few actions are available to *keep* it from raining (short of requesting divine intervention), but if there were, you would need only to know that a picnic would be no fun in the rain before working on shaping actions.

The requirement to visualize the failed assumption is a distinct and important characteristic of defining hedges. It makes defining hedging actions the most labor-intensive part of ABP and, in fact, leads us to recommend a preliminary step: generating and using *worlds* (or, in the strategic planning literature of the private sector, *scenarios*). That is, one way to generate hedging actions for a vulnerable assumption would be for a small group of organizational leaders to analyze the assumption, determine the implications of its failure, and develop appropriate hedges. There are perhaps other ways. The approach we (strongly) favor is for the planners to generate a world embodying the violated assumption, to use that world to develop a general organizational response, and, finally, to define actions that are prudent.

Generating and Using Worlds

In our usage, a *world* is a hypothetical future situation in which a vulnerable assumption has been violated for one (or more) of the plausible reasons identified in Step 2. Such a world is not complete in the sense that it describes how every aspect of today's world has evolved. It is intended only to add to the plausibility of evolving from today's world into one in which the vulnerable assumption has changed. Examples of such worlds are common;[1] details here will be kept to a minimum. Basically, the world should have as much detail as is needed to make the violation vivid to the developers of the responses, because the primary goal of this step is to explore the consequences of the violated assumption to the organization. Consider again, for example, a world in which the assumption that our long-range weapons systems are no longer effective is realized. If the organization is concerned with the counters that must be developed to restore the effectiveness of those systems, the details of the systems that bring about the violation are important to include. On the other hand, if the organization is concerned with what changes must be made to operational doctrine, the technological details of the counters are less important than the implications of being unable to set up conditions for decisive engagement.

The arguments for using worlds preparatory to defining hedging actions are more experiential than logical. That is, using worlds is a creative enterprise. The more vivid the hypothetical situation can be made, the more productive is the environment it creates. And the greater is the involvement of a variety of people with different points of view, the more salutary are the effects of that variety. The world itself encourages a contemplation of how it could evolve from today's world and often suggests additional signposts.

Conceiving Responses

Hedging actions are a part of the general process of devising responses for an organization *as though* an important assumption had become invalid. In ABP,

---

[1]Schwartz, 1991, pp. 47–60.

a *response* is an idea or concept[2] for dealing with an importantly changed world and the primary actions required to implement it.

The appropriate response could be relatively minor or revolutionary, depending on the nature of the (presumed) violated assumption. In the extreme it could lead to an idea or concept for the complete restructuring of the organization. Responses should meet the following criteria:

- They must be relevant to the world for which they are designed.

- They should also be feasible in the sense that they are achievable by the organization and that the general actions required for their implementation can be laid out.

For any given world there is likely to be a variety of reasonable organizational responses—none of which can be spelled out in detail without further details about the world itself. The goal in this preliminary step is not to get the details of a single response right but to explore appropriate responses. If there is a consensus response from the planners, so much the better. More likely, there will be more than one response, each with significant merit, and the primary actions to carry out the response should be identified for each. The question of the right number of responses is part of a larger practical issue that is discussed in "Practical Considerations" of this chapter.

Devising responses should form the basis of the debate on the organization's "best" response to a given world and its embodied violated assumption. It involves considerable judgment and creativity, and the responses will only be as good as the judgment and creativity that go into them.

From these organizational responses and their associated actions are gleaned those actions that should be taken today to preserve the organization's options in the face of uncertainty about the assumption's failing. Those actions to be taken today are the hedging actions.

---

[2]The word *concept* is closest in dictionary meaning to what we intend here, but it carries a somewhat different connotation in common Army usage; it has been paired here with *idea* to avoid confusion.

ILLUSTRATIONS

Army 21

Four assumptions of Army 21 were identified as vulnerable to events in the next 25–30 years. To facilitate developing hedging actions for those vulnerabilities, a world was built around each negated assumption to contemplate the kind of actions the Army could prudently take to deal with the failed assumption. For the Army 21 effort, we developed a rough outline of each of the four worlds as a lead-in for the three-day TRADOC-run workshop to ensure that the design of the responses to the worlds was informed by a broad collection of military expertise and experience. The goals of the workshop were to expand the details of the worlds as necessary to develop responses, then to develop shaping and hedging actions and signposts appropriate for each of the worlds.

A good example of the process at this point is the world in which the violated assumption is, again, that the United States continues to play a primary role in maintaining global stability across the operational continuum. In this world, the U.S. Army is no longer the pre-eminent "cop on the block." American dominance of the world political scene slowly dissipates through a combination of events and policy choices: domestic pressures on the budget, decreased industrial competitiveness, pressures from multinationals to redefine the concept of national interest, and the ascendance of the United Nations.

In particular, the United Nations calls upon the U.S. Navy and Air Force but uses now-capable regional armies for land operations in its international peacekeeping missions. The U.S. Army of this world finds itself relegated to a minor role in overseas ventures and in domestic budgets.

The workshop participants saw the Army as being generally much more involved in domestic affairs, including combating drugs and/or civil disorders, undertaking border-police actions, and acting as a national training-and-education agency. They redesigned the Army into three parts: a small (3–5 divisions) combat force that could be used to project power abroad, a large coterie of reserve personnel devoted to domestic assistance and training programs, and a portion of the active-duty force devoted to training and maintaining the National Guard and Reserves. They designed a rotation of the officer corps among the three major components and laid out the primary missions of each component. They then described the actions necessary to move from today's Army to their new concept, identified shaping actions that could be taken today to bring that world about (it being deemed preferable to today's world), hedging actions, and signposts that were deemed compelling evidence that a world of this type was coming about.

Royal Dutch/Shell

In the first Royal Dutch/Shell example (Chapter Four), Shell was looking at a decision to build a multibillion-dollar platform to extract natural gas from the Troll gas field in the North Atlantic. In the "Greening of Russia" scenario, the Soviet Union would be trying to compete in the European natural-gas market and trying to drop the 35-percent ceiling the Europeans had placed on natural gas that could be purchased from the Soviet Union. As a consequence, the price of gas would be driven down and would reduce the economic viability of the Troll platform. Shell recognized that if OPEC's (Organization of Petroleum Exporting Countries) unity collapsed, demand for oil in an age of increasing conservation and energy efficiency could dwindle.

Because of the plausibility of this scenario, Shell took several hedging actions. One was making an extra effort to bring down the cost of the Troll platform project. Two others, not overinvesting in new oil fields nor purchasing other oil companies at premium prices, went counter to the trend of the late 1970s, a time when oil prices had been high for nearly 10 years and other firms were "drilling on Wall Street," by buying oil companies at high prices to gain their oil fields. When oil prices fell, Shell was in a much better position than other oil companies and was able to buy oil reserves at half the price that had been available six months before.

Furthermore, as Schwartz explains, Shell continued to ask the right questions and take appropriate actions. As oil prices began to fluctuate more wildly than at any time prior to World War II, Shell challenged the assumption that they would settle down again and came up with a scenario in which oil and gasoline became commodities on the international market, and trading in oil, as do commodities investors, might be a good business. Designing a trading system to take advantage of such a change generally takes years, but the scenario was sufficiently vivid to enable Shell to envision the usefulness of such a system. Shell began to design a trading system, and by the time the price of oil collapsed, it was in operation.

PRACTICAL CONSIDERATIONS

Handling the Combinatorial Explosion[3] Problem

Throughout Assumption-Based Planning, there is the potential for the number of entities generated in a given step to overwhelm the planning system. In the first two steps, we have recommended erring on the side of inclusion in identifying important assumptions and their vulnerabilities. In this, Step 5, responses are developed for assumption–vulnerability pairs and there are two logically distinct ways in which too many such deliberations can be called for:

1. For completeness, a response is generated for each of the $2^M - 1$ combinations of failed assumptions, where M is the total number of assumption–vulnerability pairs.

2. Developing responses to each assumption–vulnerability pair overwhelms the planning system, either because there are too many pairs or because too many distinct responses have been generated for the various pairs.

The first complication is dealt with systemically. That is, in ABP, we declare that dealing with each pair in isolation is sufficient and that dealing with any larger combinations of pairs paralyzes the analysis unnecessarily. This specific guidance on reducing combinatorial explosion is the single largest factor in reducing the overall number of potential analyzable situations (from $2^M - 1$ to M). One can argue that some combinations of violated assumptions can have important

---

[3] *Combinatorial explosion* derives from the logical combinations available to a number of assumption vulnerabilities. If there are M vulnerable assumptions, there are $2^M - 1$ different logical combinations of worlds that could have violated assumptions in them. This geometric factor is the explosion. Combinatorial explosion is a common planning problem but is not often dealt with explicitly. Perhaps the most explicit method for dealing with the problem (in pairwise comparisons) is the cross-impact matrix. See, for example, Ayres, R. U., *Technological Forecasting and Long-Range Planning*, New York: McGraw-Hill, 1969, and Martino, J. P., *Technological Forecasting for Decisionmaking*, New York: Elsevier, 1972.

synergistic effects that should be explored, but we take the position that the benefit of doing so before the fact is outweighed by the practical impossibility of doing so for all possible combinations. If a specific combination of violated assumptions can be shown clearly to have effects requiring special consideration, such consideration is certainly appropriate but should be the exception and not the rule: Such combinations can overwhelm the execution of ABP.

The second complication is a variation of the problems in earlier steps of how many is too many. Here, however, the answer differs from those of Steps 1 and 2 because of the amount of work involved in producing thoughtful organizational responses to a given assumption–vulnerability pair. Only a relatively small target number of assumption–vulnerability pairs can reasonably be carried through exhaustive response development.

We recommend reducing the list of pairs before detailed responses are developed by performing an approximate "cost–risk" assessment, which carries risk from Step 2 and associates with it the cost of generating the response relative to that risk. That is, for a given assumption–vulnerability pair, some judgment must be made about the nominal "cost" of generating a response to that pair. Immediate attention may then be restricted to those responses that would be least damaging to the organization's plans, i.e., responses with the lowest cost-to-risk ratio. If an inordinate number of pairs have very low ratios, leadership may have to increase the planning staff to handle all of them. Otherwise, the remainder may be deferred to future planning cycles.

This last point about deferment to later planning cycles is an important one. A large number of assumption–vulnerability pairs can also be winnowed by exploring the most urgent subset during the first planning cycle and additional subsets during subsequent cycles. If the time horizon is sufficiently far out, there is likely to be enough lead time to allow a more leisurely pace in exploring a large set of pairs.

How Many Worlds?

The frequently asked question of how many worlds should be generated must be qualified by saying that ABP does not strictly require the use of worlds in order to develop responses. We have strongly recommended using them because of their evocative characteristics. If worlds are used during Step 5, this question is the same as that about the number of assumption–vulnerability pairs for which detailed responses should be developed. Perhaps the best answer is the number of worlds and/or assumption–vulnerability pairs that can comfortably be accommodated by the planning organization. Experience in strategic planning in the business world suggests that more than six alternative worlds or pairs[4] become unwieldy and fewer than three tend to suggest a lack of creativity on the part of the planners.

The number of generated worlds should most properly depend on the purpose of the planning process. One planning situation may demand rigorous rationale and be served best by using only worlds that are very plausible and defensible from today's characteristics and trends. That situation could lead to as few as two worlds. Another planning situation may be exploratory and intended to suggest the breadth of uncertainty facing an organization, leading to a dozen or more merely possible worlds that best serve that intent.

When to Implement a Hedging Action

Practical consideration of timing on hedging actions is completely analogous to that of shaping actions. The discussion at the end of Chapter Five applies equally well.

In addition, however, the implementation of hedging actions has a more subtle aspect: A poorly handled hedging action can weaken shaping actions. The classical example is confrontation with a wild animal. The correct shaping action is to hold your ground and look fierce. If, as a hedging action, you begin backing away (to give yourself a headstart if the animal attacks), that very hedging action may invite the attack that your shaping action is trying to prevent. At times it may be necessary either to develop hedging actions in absolute secrecy or even to avoid developing (overtly) such actions until it becomes clear that associated shaping actions are failing. The latter will depend on signposts. The dependence of these ABP products and the ordering of the five steps are discussed in Chapter Seven.

---

[4]Schwartz, 1991, pp. 47–60.

ORDERING OF THE ABP STEPS

As presented in this report, the steps of the Assumption-Based Planning process have a certain sequence that must be followed to a given end. In this chapter, we clarify the logical dependence of one step on another and clarify the possibility of performing a complete process using as few as two steps.

LOGICAL DEPENDENCE

Ordering the five Assumption-Based Planning steps sequentially tends to imply a logical dependence of each step on all the preceding steps. As Figure 7.1 shows, such is not the case. Identifying the vulnerabilities of the assumptions in Step 2 depends logically on first having identified the important assumptions. Once the assumptions and their vulnerabilities, or failure mechanisms, have been identified, however, there is enough information to proceed with any one or all of the remaining three steps.

The signposts of Step 3 are an indication that an assumption is becoming more vulnerable or is failing. Dependent only on the assumptions and their associated vulnerabilities, signposts are independent of any actions to be taken in the event they are observed.

Shaping actions, which depend only on the assumptions and their associated failure mechanisms, are intended to exert what control the organization has over the vulnerability of those assumptions. By definition, most shaping actions, if they are not already ongoing, should be initiated immediately. For example, once a military plan is

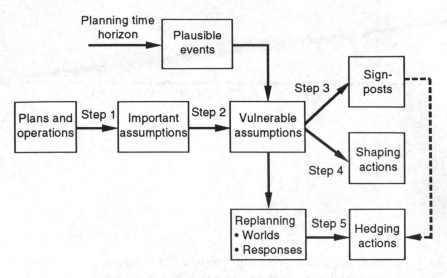

Figure 7.1—ABP Steps and Logical Dependence

dependent on the primacy of a particular technology, shaping actions are generally taken immediately to ensure that the technology cannot be countered or that counters can be defeated. It is generally too late to begin counter-counter shaping actions once the first countermeasures to the technology appear.

On the other hand, after the signposts have been identified, it is possible that further shaping actions based on those signposts may be definable. Such an example is establishing diplomatic relations with Latvia, a shaping action that might be designed to assist in breaking up the Soviet Union as a superpower. Taking that action before the appearance of serious cracks in the Soviet empire (such as the fall of the Berlin Wall), however, might have been counterproductive. Thus, there may be some value in waiting to execute shaping actions until after the signposts have been established.

Defining the hedging actions for a given vulnerable assumption requires that the assumption and a failure mechanism have been established (Steps 1 and 2) and that an intermediate step of planning for the world in which that assumption has failed ("Replanning" in the figure) has been taken. In the world of the violated assumption, whether the signposts have been observed or the shaping actions have had the desired effect is immaterial. The planning that must be done to establish hedging actions is independent of the signposts and shaping actions defined in Steps 3 and 4.

Hedging actions, on the other hand, are those actions that should be taken *before* the world of the violated assumption is projected to come about, to preserve organizational options or to prepare for that world. The definition of those actions (i.e., the "what to do") is independent of signposts, but the execution of those actions (the "when to do them") may not be. Indeed, hedging actions that are very disruptive to current operations may require clear evidence that the assumption is failing (or has failed) before they can be implemented.

The hedging actions that are of greatest interest to programmers and budgeteers are those that should be taken independent of signposts, because they need to be incorporated into current programs and budgets. *When* to do hedging actions is more likely to be tied to signposts than when to do shaping actions. Further, if the warning that hedging actions should be initiated could come at any time, it is important to identify those actions. The broken line in Figure 7.1 shows this logical-dependence aspect of Step 5 on Step 3.

PARTIAL ASSUMPTION-BASED PLANNING

Although Steps 3 through 5 are usually logically independent, there *is* a purpose behind ordering them as we have. In fact, there is a dimension, or continuum, along which all the steps form a properly ordered sequence. Furthermore, the sequence along that dimension has practical consequences.

The dimension is defined by its two endpoints. At one end is "how to think" about the future; at the other end is "what to do" about the future. As ordered, the steps of ABP move from the how-to-think end toward the what-to-do end. Identifying the organization's important assumptions in Step 1 is the starting point for how to think about the future, but is also focused entirely on understanding the organization and contains nothing about what to do. Identifying the vulnerabilities to the organization's assumptions continues the process of thinking about the organization, but brings the first intimations that something might have to be done.

The signposts in Step 3 are the next level in thinking about the future—paying attention to what is happening in time. Monitoring the signposts is the first action that should be taken. Shaping actions are potentially expensive and disruptive actions the organization should take in order to protect its current plan or operations. And, finally, the hedging actions of Step 5 require deliberately restructuring the organization (conceptually) for worlds that render its current plan or operations inappropriate.

There is a movement throughout the steps of ABP, as ordered, from understanding the problem toward solving it, so that ABP can be halted anywhere in the process, depending on the objectives and planning style of the organization. For example, in an organization with a strong visionary leader, it may be sufficient to go through the first two steps of ABP and present the leader with the current assumptions and vulnerabilities, or go through the first three steps. Those steps would provide enough information for the leader to develop a vision for the organization from which further planning and programming would stem. Going through all five steps is more compatible in an organization with a more decentralized or consensual approach to planning.

The most time- and labor-intensive step in ABP is likely to be Step 5, with its alternative worlds and replanning. Step 5 is also the epitome of planning in that it contemplates worlds that are unexpected or undesirable. The contemplation and preparation for those worlds are what do the most to reduce the risks in the organization's future. Nonetheless, an admittedly riskier but quicker or less-expensive approach to planning could eliminate this last step during a given planning cycle.

Finally, there are practical advantages to identifying an organization's important assumptions (that is, stopping after Step 1) that may have very little to do with planning. Understanding an organization's fundamental assumptions is key to understanding the organization itself. Both public and private sectors put a high premium on establishing organizational identities for purposes that range far beyond planning.

Chapter Eight

ASSUMPTION-BASED PLANNING IN A PLANNING SYSTEM

To date, Assumption-Based Planning has been applied primarily in support of two separate plans that were generated as part of a larger planning system, the Army Long-Range Planning System. For this reason, the role of ABP in the overall Army long-range plan or planning system received little attention. It follows, then, that we would ask what the role of ABP is in a larger planning system.

This question has both a practical and a theoretical aspect. The practical aspect involves working actively with a specific planning system and exploring the utility of ABP for that system. We are currently assisting the Deputy Chief of Staff for Operations to update the Army regulation (AR 11-32) that defines the Army Long-Range Planning System. One of the elements of that assistance is to explore how and where ABP should fit into the structure and execution of Army long-range planning. That work is ongoing at this writing and will be reported on separately when completed.

The more theoretical aspect of the question involves thinking about the capabilities and limitations of ABP and assessing its role in a generalized hierarchical planning system. That aspect is discussed next.

WHERE ABP BEST FITS IN THE PLANNING SYSTEM

A sufficiently complex organization, such as the military or a large industry, plans at several levels in a hierarchy, either for different purposes (e.g., operational and strategic) or at different time horizons (e.g., short, mid, and long range). Commonalities across such planning systems include key players and organizations responsible for planning at each echelon of the hierarchy, policies and procedures (e.g., scheduling, cycling, formats), a set of planning activities, planning guidance, and products. For our purposes, we are interested in only two elements of such a planning system: the organizational hierarchy on which it is overlaid and the focus of the planning. The coordinates in Figure 8.1 are a simplified representation of those elements. The vertical axis represents the planning echelon in the hierarchy, and the horizontal axis represents the time-horizon focus. The horizontal axis is doubly labeled to indicate the two major types of planning focus evident in the literature. Such labeling is *not* intended to draw an exact comparison between the two.

As a planning tool, ABP should be applicable to every plan developed anywhere in a hierarchical planning system, because every plan or subplan is based on a set of explicit and implicit assumptions, and those assumptions are subject to vulnerability testing with ABP.

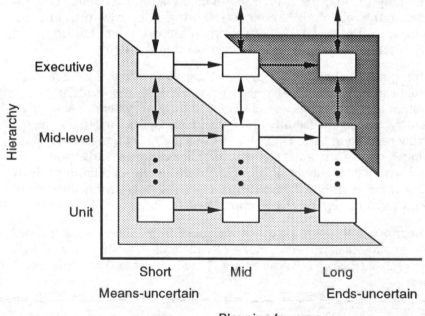

Figure 8.1—Hierarchical Planning System

It is *not* always true that ABP will be able to improve a plan. In Chapter Three (and Appendix A), we discuss how ABP has been more appropriately aimed at ends-uncertain planning environments. This would mean that ABP is a more appropriate tool the farther to the right one is in the planning system of Figure 8.1.

Similarly, the lower a planner is in the planning hierarchy, the more means dominated the planning tends to be; that is, the directions will be more specific and detailed from higher levels and the planning tasks will be more specific. We can infer, then, that ends-uncertainty is much more the concern of higher echelons in the organization, which suggests that ABP is more appropriate closer to the top of the hierarchy.

A general point can now be made about the utility of Assumption-Based Planning:

> *The utility of ABP is greater the higher in the organization and the farther out in time or uncertainty that organization is looking.*

Although ABP may be applied to any plan generated in a planning system, it is more beneficial the closer it is to the upper right-hand (dark-shaded) corner of the planning system in Figure 8.1, an interesting area to contemplate in the planning world.

This "corner" in private industry is where strategic planning takes place. Strategic planning deals with the ends the organization should strive for in the future—the ends-uncertain and long-range part of the planning spectrum.[1] Furthermore, experience has taught the private sector that strategic planning is an activity that should be carried out only at the highest levels of the organization.[2] The military once mirrored this hierarchy. Before 1989, long-range planning in the Army was the primary domain of the Office of the Army Chief of Staff (in fact, the 1989 regulation that spells out the Long-Range

---

[1]Please refer to Appendix B for a discussion of long-range, strategic, and ends-uncertain planning.

[2]See, for example, Kukalis, Sal, "Strategic Planning in Large U.S. Corporations—A Survey," *Omega—International Journal of Management Science*, Vol. 16, No. 5, 1988, pp. 393–404, and Wilson, Ian, "The State of Strategic Planning—What Went Wrong? What Goes Right?" *Technology Forecasting and Social Change*, Vol. 37, 1990, pp. 103–110.

Planning System was adapted from a Chief-of-Staff document that described the earlier long-range planning system).

In ABP terms, the upper right-hand area of the figure is where the actual products of ABP—actions—predominate. That is, the farther out we go on the figure, the more likely it is that assumptions will fail. Plans coming out of the upper right-hand corner of Figure 8.1 will thus be more focused on those actions that must be taken today in order to hedge or shape against a vulnerable assumption's breaking.

A final ABP-related point to be made about the upper right-hand corner of the figure is that changes in the world can broaden the dark-shaded area of the figure in which ABP is most beneficial. One can argue that this has happened since 1987 for the Army. That is, in 1987, that ends-uncertain area was restricted to the very long range and the very highest levels in the Army. Changes that have occurred in Europe since 1987 have brought great uncertainty in Army planning much farther to the left in Figure 8.1 and have increased the dark-shaded area of the figure in which ABP is of apparent utility. ABP is being viewed in the Army as a tool for mid-range and even short-range planning in these newly uncertain times.

WHEN BEST TO APPLY ABP

We have said that ABP is applicable to any plan, but more applicable to plans higher in the planning hierarchy and farther out in time and uncertainty. Plan quality also determines the applicability of ABP in a planning system:

> Assumption-Based Planning is more beneficial the more complete and realistic the plans (subplans) are to which it is applied.

We describe an early stage of the *Army Modernization Memorandum* (AMM) to illustrate this point.

The AMM is TRADOC's comprehensive, constrained modernization strategy for Army materiel. In its early stage, the AMM process generates a cost-unconstrained, rank-ordered list of all pertinent modernization actions the Army should contemplate. That list is a plan in the sense that, if cost were not a factor, the Army would want to implement all of its elements. We applied ABP to this "plan" with unsatisfactory results: In thinking about the plan, we concluded that it merely represented that the people responsible for this product had done an important part of their job well. The assumptions we identified were very general and inclusive, and the elements in the rank-ordered list did a creditable job of covering materiel modernization for just about anything that could happen in the future. One could argue with the actual rank-ordering, but if cost truly were not a factor, the rank-ordering would be immaterial. We had discovered that a resource-unconstrained plan is not a good candidate for ABP application.

Therefore, until the difficult choices have been made in a plan (or planning process), important assumptions cannot be revealed. Even when the plan is properly resource-constrained, it is unlikely to reveal all of its assumptions clearly; rarely is a coherent set of criteria applied in the complex process of making trade-offs. Doing so in that process generally leads to a farragolike plan that represents a variety of (perhaps even conflicting) assumptions. ABP's value lies, in part, in being able to winnow out from that farrago not only the explicit assumptions the plan is making about the world, but the more subtle, implicit assumptions that have resulted from the options taken and those forgone.

In conclusion, whereas ABP is more beneficial the higher up in the organization and the farther out in outcome uncertainty it is applied, it is more beneficial the more complete the plan is. There is clearly a tension here. Plans that come from the upper right-hand corner of Figure 8.1 are much less detailed than those from the lower left-hand corner. Consequently, we must emphasize that detail is not what makes a plan a good or bad candidate for ABP application, but rather how close to implementation it is.

A plan that is ready for implementation or that has been implemented is a good candidate for ABP application because it represents all the resource constraints required by its level in the planning hierarchy. It is as detailed as it need be for that level of planning—the crucial factor.

Let us look again, then, at a different phase of the AMM: after the AMM rank-ordered list of modernization elements had been cost-constrained and had been reviewed and adjusted by the various agencies that had oversight responsibility for it. At this point it was a much different plan, representing a much narrower view of what will be important in the future. It is at this point that the AMM was ready for application of Assumption-Based Planning.

Chapter Nine

CONCLUDING REMARKS

Assumption-Based Planning is not a panacea. It does not purport to reveal truth about the uncertain future; it cannot replace creative thinking with formulaic certitude; it does not obviate critical judgments. Planning under great uncertainty will only be as good as the insight and care of the people doing that planning. What the methodology *does* is provide a systematic way of thinking about a future containing fundamental uncertainties about an organization's ends and a framework for, over time, dealing explicitly with those uncertainties.

As specified at the beginning of this report, Assumption-Based Planning does not provide a plan as much as a process. The *process* of Assumption-Based Planning has two important benefits. The first benefit is that by consciously excluding the no-violated-assumptions part of planning that is most ends-"certain," ABP lays bare the uncertainties in ends at the planning horizon that might otherwise be given scant attention—ends that should be the first priority in an ends-uncertain planning environment.

The second benefit is that ABP focuses decisionmaking on near-term actions rather than on a long, detailed plan for an uncertain future. It is common for long-range (hence, ends-uncertain) plans to posit a single world containing all the known threats (a "worst-case" world) and then present a detailed plan for handling that world out to the planning horizon. Such an approach distributes the detailed plan relatively evenly across the planning time period—a period with increasing uncertainty about the world. By paying attention first to near-term actions and signposts, ABP concentrates its outputs on those decisions that come nearest in time and leaves the details of, and decisions on, future actions to be made when the ends are less uncertain. In this way, Assumption-Based Planning, as a process, invites an ends-uncertain plan to contain near-term actions (through the planning cycle) and signposts as the plan, in place of the more common detailed plan out to the end of the planning horizon. This is a very different way of looking at ends-uncertain plans, as detailed in Chapter Eight.

The practice of Assumption-Based Planning involves a certain kind of thinking that is beneficial for ends-uncertain planning. As a tool it also generates products. In this role it provides two further benefits: a systematic basis for testing plans or operations for planning failure, and a specific mechanism for dealing with ends-uncertainty over time. To the extent that organizational failures can arise from violated assumptions, a careful, systematic identification of the important assumptions an organization makes and an equally careful identification of those assumptions that are vulnerable within the planning period should go a long way toward avoiding planning failures.

The hedging and shaping actions and signposts provide a specific mechanism for dealing with ends-uncertainties over time. The signposts provide the essential power to this benefit, because they are associated with a specific assumption and provide an indication that that assumption's vulnerability is changing. By also "tying" the hedging and shaping actions to a specific assumption, change in an assumption's vulnerability leads directly to the actions that should be changed. In this way, as ends-uncertainties dissipate over time, it is clear which actions need to be altered. In sharp contrast is the planning for a worst-case world that is the common "fix" to the trend-based approach for planning in ends-uncertain environments. In that worst-case world, all the assumption vulnerabilities are lumped together. If one assumption vulnerability changes, there is no way to determine which of the prescribed actions to change except by reinitiating the planning process.

Nothing done in the short term can "prove" the efficacy of a planning methodology; nor can the monitoring, over time, of a single instance of a plan generated by that methodology, unless there is a competing parallel plan. The more general test of a planning methodology is whether planners find it a useful tool for their planning problems. By that measure, Assumption-Based Planning has been a success. It has been used for planning in the Army doctrine and personnel communities and is being studied for use in the materiel and intelligence communities. It is being considered in the updating of the *Army Long-Range Planning System* (AR 11-32). ABP has also attracted interest outside the Army community, but only recently; therefore, its utility in that arena, while promising, remains moot at this time.

ASSUMPTION-BASED PLANNING AND TIME HORIZONS

It is common for an organization to undertake planning exercises to guide its operations in the light of potential future events. Such planning is typically structured to consider events within a specific time period, or out to a specific time horizon. In the past, separate planning exercises were labeled by time horizons—typically short, medium, and long range.

Time horizons are important in planning because they define the intended duration of the plan. Time horizons often determine what type of planning approach is taken. The important distinction is not time, however, but the type of uncertainty the organization faces within a given time horizon.

The types of uncertainty are most easily seen at two extreme ends of the planning spectrum. If a large organization, such as the Army, were to make plans for next month, the goals of the planning would be very clear, the future quite predictable, and the planning would be focused on selecting the proper means of achieving the goals. At this extreme, the organization's assumptions about how the world will evolve are complete and solid, and the selection of available, appropriate planning tools is large, depending on the exact nature of the means-uncertain planning in this environment.

At the other extreme, if the Army were to plan for the year 2050, its assumptions about the future world will be very incomplete and/or tenuous. Here, even the goals, or ends, of the planning are unclear. Assumption-Based Planning is more appropriate in this environment. At the extremes are two distinctly different planning environments calling for distinctly different planning strategies.

The crossover point between predominantly means-uncertain planning and predominantly ends-uncertain planning is not a constant function of time. Recent history provides a good example. For much of the past 40 years, the military has planned with the reasonable certainty that the Soviet Union was the dominant threat and would continue to be for 10 to 20 years into the future. Therefore, most planning fell within an environment of means-uncertainty. Ends-uncertain planning was much farther out in time, usually 25 years or more. Today, however, significant ends-uncertainty exists in time horizons that were once predominantly means-uncertain.

EXTENT OF THE ENDS-UNCERTAIN TIME FRAME

The time frame over which ends-uncertainty affects Assumption-Based Planning has both near and far boundaries. Each boundary is determined by different considerations.

For the near boundary, ABP could be used to deal with even the nearest and slightest uncertainty. However, other, simpler, tools, such as trend extrapolation, may offer easier and equally sound methods for short-range planning. The near boundary is probably best set subjectively and arbitrarily as the nearest future time at which the planner feels uncomfortable with other methods of addressing uncertainty surrounding his or her important assumptions. In practical terms, the *near time boundary* of ABP is determined by the earliest time any important assumption is deemed vulnerable to the sort of uncertainty other planning methods cannot reduce. There is no need to use ABP closer to the present than the time when the first assumption is considered vulnerable and the outcome of its vulnerability cannot be plausibly predicted as a single event.

The far boundary at which ABP is appropriate is more complicated to set. It is not simply the time at which the assumption with the most distant vulnerability appears threatened. Planners need not plan so far out that plausible events in distant years require no action today. Instead, the far horizon is limited by that time needed by the planners to prepare for future assumption-violating events. Hence, the *far time boundary* need not extend beyond the longest time required to prepare for any of the plausibly violated assumptions.

Preparations take three forms: monitoring (establishing and watching signposts), hedging, and shaping. Because preparations cost money, it is important to know when to begin each action. For each vulnerable assumption, the planner works backward from the earliest plausible failing of the assumption to an estimate of how long it would take to shape the world to a desired state or to hedge against plausible outcomes.

Deciding whether to shape or hedge depends on whether the planning organization has the ability to shape; if it does, the decision then rests on relative costs and outcomes of shaping and hedging. Regardless of whether shaping or hedging is selected, planners must estimate how long the action will take. If the action can be completed in less time than the estimated time to the failing of the assumption, there is no need to begin it today. Instead, the planner may wish to establish one or more signposts to warn of conditions that indicate the approach of a violated assumption.

Once a signpost announces the approach of a violated assumption, the planning organization must decide when to initiate the hedging and/or shaping action. Such action must obviously be initiated far enough in advance to complete the action before the assumption is expected to fail. If signposts fail to warn of the failure's approach before the minimum time required to act, then, upon reaching that minimum time, the planning organization will initiate a hedging or shaping action without the warning. Prudent planning requires, in fact, that hedging and shaping funds be earmarked in the organization's fiscal documents. For example, if the planning organization estimates that an assumption will fail, or be violated, in the year 2000, and it will take five years to act, then the organization should this year include hedging funds in the 1995 column of its financial plans (in Army planning, this would be the *Program Objectives Memorandum* [POM] and the *Future-Years Defense Program* [FYDP]).

The far time boundary of ABP, then, varies from time to time and is set by the longest lead time required to complete any anticipated hedging or shaping action.

As an illustration, suppose a planning organization has identified all its important and plausibly vulnerable assumptions and determined that all appear sound or reasonably predictable out to 10 years; the range across all assumptions runs from 10 to 25 years. The near time horizon for ABP in that organization is 10 years. We know nothing yet about the far time horizon.

Suppose further that the organization has arrayed its assumptions by earliest vulnerability (10–25 years) and has decided on hedging and/or shaping actions to deal with each. Let us say that the assumption with the longest viability (25 years) requires a hedging or shaping action that can be completed in eight years, that is, beginning 17 years away. Since no action is required today, the vulnerability of that assumption lies outside the ABP planning horizon.

Another assumption may have a more immediate planning horizon: an assumption whose viability is 20 years and for which hedging is deemed the best action, but whose hedge would also require 20 years to complete. The existence of these conditions sets the far time boundary (for planning related to that assumption) at 20 years, the minimum time required to complete the appropriate action. Once this process is repeated for all vulnerable assumptions, the organization can set its far time boundary, which equals the longest time required to complete any appropriate action that must begin today.

SELECTING THE TIME HORIZON

As suggested in Chapter Three, the time horizon for identifying the vulnerability of assumptions can be established in two ways: by leadership fiat or by the planning organization. Set the first way, the horizon can either be fixed or tentative. A tentative setting means that the leadership may not have a clear horizon in mind but may fix one to begin the ABP process. During the ABP process, planners can be watchful for vulnerable assumptions beyond the tentative horizon. If any are discovered, planners would notify the leadership and recommend adjustment of the horizon. Similarly, within the tentative horizon, planners might find no plausibly vulnerable assumptions that require action now. If so, they might recommend shortening the horizon to the point at which at least one assumption requires action today.

If the planning organization selects the horizon on its own, that horizon would be taken somewhere in the ends-uncertain time frame as established above and depending on purpose.

ASSUMPTION-BASED PLANNING AND OTHER PLANNING TOOLS

Assumption-Based Planning was originally intended to be an improvement on what we call trend-based planning, for planning in times of great uncertainty. Its primary rationale thus rests on its merits relative to trend-based planning. On the other hand, ABP is a planning tool with describable characteristics and can be compared with general planning tools from other arenas. The first section below addresses the strengths and weaknesses of ABP in relation to trend-based planning. The second section briefly addresses how ABP compares with strategic planning tools from the business world.

ABP AND TREND-BASED PLANNING

ABP was developed in response to shortcomings of the trend-based planning approach, the method used by the Army. A common method for planning, the trend-based approach is summarized in Figure B.1. Planning with this methodology tends to produce a future world (or worlds) with high descriptive plausibility and a clear transition from today's world to the projected world or worlds. Trend-based planning can be thought of as an "outside–in" approach to planning: Its initial focus is on events that are likely to occur in the outside world, and its subsequent focus is the potential effects of those events on the organization or object of interest.

The trend-based approach is a good foundation for planning when the "most-likely" world from trend-based projections has, say, a

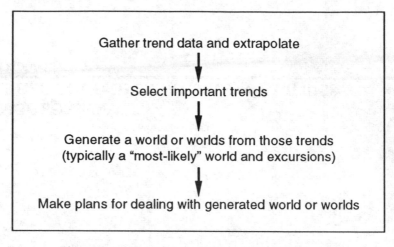

Figure B.1—Major Steps in Trend-Based Planning

50 percent or greater chance of eventuating. However, planning in times of great ends-uncertainty tends to produce trend-projected worlds with probabilities much smaller than 50 percent, worlds likely to produce a risky plan and therefore a bad foundation for planning. In the business world, risks are acceptable under many circumstances, whereas, in national security planning, strategic risks are anathema. Hence, the trend-based approach is dangerous.

Before arguing that the assumption-based approach is an improvement for planning in times of significant ends-uncertainty, we must emphasize that the products of ABP—vulnerable assumptions, signposts, shaping actions, potential organizational responses, and hedging actions—do *not* constitute a plan. That is, the output of Assumption-Based Planning is not a *complete* plan. Clearly, the ABP products are useful inputs to a plan, but a plan would also include, for example, those actions that should be taken in the case that *none* of the assumptions has failed out to the planning horizon (although the farther out the time horizon is, the less important that case might be). This issue has been excluded from Assumption-Based Planning and left for the larger planning *system* of which ABP is intended to be a part. This aspect of ABP is discussed in Chapter Eight.

Theoretically, it would be a relatively simple matter to include the no-violated-assumption plan into the definition of Assumption-Based Planning and have it produce plans. The primary motivation behind ABP, however, was not to produce plans but to think about ends-uncertain planning in a different way. The no-violated-assumption plan offers a good segue into what we mean by thinking a different way.

With no violated assumptions, there is little reason to change the planning ends. If the ends remain unchanged, the planning involved becomes basically means-uncertain planning. In typical means-uncertain planning, the challenge is to devise the best means for achieving the ends and the plan for implementing those means. Such plans contain great detail about schedules and materiel. In ends-uncertain situations, such detailed plans are inappropriate because they threaten the contemplation of alternative ends. It was, therefore, a conscious decision to exclude the no-violated-assumptions plan from Assumption-Based Planning.

This exclusion brings into sharper focus two benefits of the *process* of Assumption-Based Planning. The first benefit is that by consciously excluding the no-violated-assumptions part of planning that is most ends-"certain," ABP lays bare the uncertainties in ends at the planning horizon that might otherwise be given scant attention—ends that should be the first priority in an ends-uncertain planning environment.

The second benefit is that ABP focuses decisionmaking on near-term actions rather than on a long, detailed plan for an uncertain future. It is common for long-range (hence, ends-uncertain) plans to posit a single world containing all the known threats (a "worst-case" world) and then present a detailed plan for handling that world out to the planning horizon. Such an approach distributes the detailed plan relatively evenly across the planning time period—a period with increasing uncertainty about the world. By paying attention first to near-term actions and signposts, ABP concentrates its outputs on those decisions that come nearest in time and leaves the details of, and decisions on, future actions to be made when the ends are less uncertain. In this way, Assumption-Based Planning, as a process, invites an ends-uncertain plan to contain near-term actions (through the planning cycle) and signposts as the plan, in place of the more common detailed plan out to the end of the planning horizon. This is a very different way of looking at ends-uncertain plans and is a topic taken up in more detail in Chapter Eight.

The practice of Assumption-Based Planning involves a certain kind of thinking that is beneficial for ends-uncertain planning. As a tool it also generates products. In this role it provides two further benefits: a systematic basis for testing plans or operations for planning failure, and a specific mechanism for dealing with ends-uncertainty over time. To the extent that organizational failures can arise from violated assumptions, a careful, systematic identification of the important assumptions an organization makes and an equally careful identification of those that are vulnerable within the planning period should go a long way toward avoiding planning failures.

The hedging and shaping actions and signposts provide a specific mechanism for dealing with ends-uncertainties over time. The signposts provide the essential power to this benefit, because they are associated with a specific assumption and provide an indication that that assumption's vulnerability is changing. By also "tying" the hedging and shaping actions to a specific assumption, change in an assumption's vulnerability leads directly to the actions that should be changed. In this way, as ends-uncertainties dissipate over time, it is clear which actions need to be altered. In sharp contrast is the planning for a worst-case world that is the common "fix" to the trend-based approach for planning in ends-uncertain environments. In that worst-case world, all the assumption vulnerabilities are lumped together. If one assumption vulnerability changes, there is no way to determine which of the prescribed actions to change except by reinitiating the planning process.

ABP AND STRATEGIC PLANNING

Assumption-Based Planning is not a totally new way of conducting long-range or ends-uncertain planning. There is extensive literature on planning, particularly in the private sector.[1] The following sub-

---

[1]For example, there is a comparison of 30 established planning tools in Webster, James, William E. Reif, and Jeffrey S. Bracker, "The Manager's Guide to Strategic

sections represent a reasonable survey of current articles on long-range and strategic planning and how they compare with ABP; they are not intended as an exhaustive search-and-compare operation. The comparisons are made according to various aspects of ABP that were chosen because they appear to best highlight differences among various methodologies described in the literature.

Long-Range Planning Versus Strategic Planning

One of the clear differences between Army long-range planning in the past and current literature on the subject is the distinction drawn between long-range planning and strategic planning. The distinction is drawn in differing ways, but one article[2] draws much the same distinction between long-range and strategic planning that we do between trend-based and Assumption-Based Planning. In its definition of *long-range planning*, the future is expected to be predictable through extrapolation of historical growth. *Strategic planning*, on the other hand, proposes that the future is not (necessarily) expected to be an improvement over the past, nor is it assumed to be an extrapolation of the past. The first step in this proposal is to identify trends, threats, opportunities, and singular "breakthrough" events that may change historical trends, events that are reminiscent of elements of change.

More generally, the distinction between long-range and strategic planning is very similar to the one we have drawn between planning based strictly on time periods and planning based on means- versus ends-uncertainty. Again, definitions vary, but strategic planning is generally associated with what we have called ends-uncertain planning.

This change from planning for short-, mid-, and long-range time periods was made long enough ago that problems have begun to

---

Planning Tools and Techniques," *Planning Review*, November/December 1989, pp. 4–13.

[2]Ansoff, Igor II., "Conceptual Underpinnings of Systematic Strategic Management," *European Journal of Operational Research*, Vol. 1, 1985, pp. 2–19.

surface with what people referred to as strategic planning.[3] Many of the problems mentioned are those we have tried to warn against in ABP—for example, strategic planning is too focused on the outside environment; single-point forecasting is inappropriate; concentrating on the "tools" of strategic planning inhibits creativity; long-range forecasts are not reliable; and strategic planning should be more about thinking than filling in boxes on a form.

Public-Sector Planning Versus Private-Sector Planning

As mentioned above, much of the literature is about planning in the private sector, and most of the public-sector literature is on governmental planning.[4] Only one article[5] dealt specifically with strategic planning and the military; it was about planning for the Canadian Armed Forces. Differences that may be expected between strategic planning in the private sector and in the public sector are worth pursuing and have not been discussed in the literature we surveyed.

The one potential difference that struck us in reading the private-sector literature is risk-taking. Many of the articles dealt explicitly or implicitly with risk-taking as a necessity in the private sector. In some cases the methodologies were geared specifically to deal with identification and assessment of risky but high-payoff opportunities. It is here that the analogy of planning in the private sector may break down in the discussion of planning for the military. At the level of force acquisition and training, the military is commanded by the *National Security Strategy* to be risk averse. Assumption-Based Planning has been designed to be risk averse in that it attempts to identify everything that could go wrong and to develop strategies to handle those possibilities. Just as risk aversion may limit the appli-

---

[3]See, for example, Ansoff, 1985, pp. 103–110; Gray, Daniel H., "Uses and Misuses of Strategic Planning," *Harvard Business Review*, Vol. 64, No. 1, 1986, pp. 89–97; and Stubbart, Charles, "Why We Need a Revolution in Strategic Planning," *Long Range Planning*, Vol. 18, No. 6, 1985, pp. 68–76.

[4]See, for example, Bryson, John M., and William D. Roering, "Initiation of Strategic Planning by Governments," *Public Administration Review*, Vol. 48, No. 6, 1988, pp. 995–1004; and Levin, Benjamin, "Squaring a Circle—Strategic Planning in Government," *Canadian Public Administration*, Vol. 28, No. 4, 1985, pp. 600–605.

[5]Russell, W. N., "Strategic Planning for the Armed Forces," *Long Range Planning*, Vol. 19, No. 4, 1986, pp. 41–46.

cability of ABP to private-sector planning, methodologies for private-sector planning may be poor analogs for strategic planning in the military because of their greater emphasis on risk-taking.

Forecasting Versus Multiple Scenarios

Strategic planning generally accepts that dealing with multiple scenarios is preferable to dealing with a single, extrapolated forecast. There is, however, a separate literature on forecasting. The question of integrating forecasting with strategic planning arises naturally, because forecasting deals with predicting the future and strategic planning deals with preplanning for the future. Gordon,[6] for example, proposes two kinds of unknown futures: an unknown but discoverable future available for analysis through appropriate research, and an intrinsically unknowable future that is not accessible by any means. In this scheme, forecasting and trend extrapolation are tools to use for discoverable futures, whereas risk analysis and multiple scenarios are tools for dealing with uncertainty in the intrinsically unknowable futures.

Baets[7] proposes a difference between operational forecasting and strategic forecasting: The former is related to operational, or means-uncertain, planning. Strategic forecasts should not be point estimates and need not be as accurate as operational forecasts.

In general, the current level of understanding of the relation between forecasting and multiple scenarios is fairly compatible with our notion that forecasts are useful tools for deciding what *could* go wrong in the future, and knowing what could go wrong is useful for generating a number of worlds to be looked at.

Multiple-Scenario Generation and Assumptions

Another issue unevenly addressed in the literature is how to generate the multiple scenarios that are to be used in strategic planning. We

---

[6]Gordon, Theodore J., "Futures Research: Did It Meet Its Promise, Can It Meet Its Promise?" *Technological Forecasting and Social Change*, Vol. 36, 1989, pp. 21–36.

[7]Baets, Walter, "Corporate Strategic Planning in an Uncertain Environment," *European Journal of Operational Research*, Vol. 32, 1986, pp. 169–181.

could find no clear instructions for generating scenarios (worlds), although there was a good deal of discussion of how multiple scenarios were to be used and, in some cases, what they should contain. Beyond the brief recognition that such scenarios should put stress on the current organization or plan in some plausible way, we found nothing akin to the ABP approach of generating scenarios from a set of vulnerable assumptions.

At least two authors dealt specifically with assumptions. Toffler[8] talks in general terms about viewing the future through re-examining one's assumptions about the world. In a very brief article, Ives[9] does a nice job of describing assumptions and suggesting their utility in strategic planning. Other authors describe understanding the "business" or key factors[10] before proceeding, approaches that are closer to using assumptions as in ABP than are the articles that specifically mention assumptions.

Shaping Actions, Hedging Actions, and Signposts

Many articles that discuss strategic planning speak only in very general terms about the products of strategic planning. In the more analytic articles, shaping and/or hedging actions are often referred to,[11] and are often used in conjunction with other descriptors. Ascher and Overholt, for example, talk about *core* and *basic strategies* with hedging strategies to handle less-likely alternatives. Generally, however, shaping and hedging actions or strategies are common ways of referring to those actions designed to change the world (to the extent possible) and to guard against unavoidable circumstances, respectively.

---

[8]Toffler, Alvin, *The Adaptive Corporation*, New York: McGraw-Hill, 1985.

[9]Ives, Jeanette R., "Articulating Values and Assumptions for Strategic Planning," *Nursing Management*, January 1991, pp. 38–39.

[10]See, for example, Huss, William R., and Edward J. Honton, "Scenario Planning: What Style Should You Use?" *Long Range Planning*, Vol. 20, No. 4, 1987, pp. 21–29; and the article by Webster, Reif, and Bracker, 1989.

[11]A canonical example of shaping and hedging actions can be found in Ascher, William, and William H. Overholt, *Strategic Planning and Forecasting: Political Risk and Economic Opportunity*, New York: John Wiley & Sons, 1983.

Signposts are less commonly found. They may become more popular, however, as a result of the influence of the Royal Dutch/Shell planners, a group that is generally conceded to be among the best strategic planning groups. The Royal Dutch/Shell group has relied heavily on the use of signposts. Schwartz[12] gives several examples in which signposts were developed from scenarios and used effectively in positioning Shell for surprises (what we would call failing assumptions) in the oil industry.

It is surprisingly uncommon to see both signposts and shaping or hedging actions together, even though they would appear to be complementary ideas: You watch for something to happen that would indicate that actions should be taken and you have developed an idea of what those actions should be. Schwartz, for example, has this in mind in talking about the utility of signposts; however, he is more concerned with using scenarios to affect the thinking of corporate planners than with the products of those scenarios. Signposts and their associated actions are part of the Shell way of strategic planning, but not as formally as suggested by ABP.

Summary of Comparisons

In short, everything in Assumption-Based Planning can be found in other long-range or strategic planning treatises, but no methodology we found is identical to it.

The two aspects of ABP that were most distinguishable from the methodologies we surveyed are its particular use of assumptions and the strong aversion to risk it embodies. As mentioned earlier, the risk aversion may be determined primarily by the nature of strategic planning in the military as distinct from that in the private sector.

ABP's distinctive use of assumptions, other than justifying the ABP name, may deserve further study. The importance of "understanding the business" is employed by the other methodologies, but appears restricted to what is assumed about the organization itself. Assumptions deal both with what is presumed about the organi-

---

[12]Schwartz, Peter, *The Art of the Long View*, New York: Doubleday Currency, 1991.

zation and what is presumed about its environment and may represent a useful extension of the notion of "understanding" for the private sector.

SELECTED BIBLIOGRAPHY

Ansoff, Igor H., "Conceptual Underpinnings of Systematic Strategic Management," *European Journal of Operational Research*, Vol. 1, 1985, pp. 2–19.

Ascher, William, and William H. Overholt, *Strategic Planning and Forecasting: Political Risk and Economic Opportunity*, New York: John Wiley & Sons, 1983.

Ayres, R. U., *Technological Forecasting and Long-Range Planning*, New York: McGraw-Hill, 1969.

Baets, Walter, "Corporate Strategic Planning in an Uncertain Environment," *European Journal of Operational Research*, Vol. 32, 1986, pp. 169–181.

Bryson, John M., and William D. Roering, "Initiation of Strategic Planning by Governments," *Public Administration Review*, Vol. 48, No. 6, 1988, pp. 995–1004.

Dalkey, Norman C., *The Delphi Method: An Experimental Study of Group Opinion*, Santa Monica, Calif.: RAND, RM-5888-PR, June 1969.

Dewar, J. A., and M. H. Levin, *Assumption-Based Planning for Army 21*, Santa Monica, Calif.: RAND, R-4172-A, 1992.

Gordon, Theodore J., "Futures Research: Did It Meet Its Promise, Can It Meet Its Promise?" *Technological Forecasting and Social Change*, Vol. 36, 1989, pp. 21–36.

Gray, Daniel H., "Uses and Misuses of Strategic Planning," *Harvard Business Review*, Vol. 64, No. 1, 1986, pp. 89–97.

Huss, William R., and Edward J. Honton, "Scenario Planning: What Style Should You Use?" *Long Range Planning*, Vol. 20, No. 4, 1987, pp. 21–29.

Ives, Jeanette R., "Articulating Values and Assumptions for Strategic Planning," *Nursing Management*, January 1991, pp. 38–39.

Kukalis, Sal, "Strategic Planning in Large U.S. Corporations—A Survey," *Omega—International Journal of Management Science*, Vol. 16, No. 5, 1988, pp. 393–404.

Levin, Benjamin, "Squaring a Circle—Strategic Planning in Government," *Canadian Public Administration*, Vol. 28, No. 4, 1985, pp. 600–605.

Martino, J. P., *Technological Forecasting for Decisionmaking*, New York: Elsevier, 1972.

Russell, W. N., "Strategic Planning for the Armed Forces," *Long Range Planning*, Vol. 19, No. 4, 1986, pp. 41–46.

Sackman, Harold, *Delphi Critique*, Lexington, Mass.: Lexington Books, 1975, p. 1.

Schwartz, Peter, *The Art of the Long View*, New York: Doubleday Currency, 1991, pp. 47–60.

Stubbart, Charles, "Why We Need a Revolution in Strategic Planning," *Long Range Planning*, Vol. 18, No. 6, 1985, pp. 68–76.

Toffler, Alvin, *The Adaptive Corporation*, New York: McGraw-Hill, 1985.

Webster, James, William E. Reif, and Jeffrey S. Bracker, "The Manager's Guide to Strategic Planning Tools and Techniques," *Planning Review*, November/December 1989, pp. 4–13.

Wilson, Ian, "The State of Strategic Planning—What Went Wrong? What Goes Right?" *Technology Forecasting and Social Change*, Vol. 37, No. 2, 1990, pp. 103–110.